One Korean's
Approach to Buddhism

SUNY series in Korean Studies

Sung Bae Park, editor

One Korean's Approach to Buddhism

The *Mom/Momjit* Paradigm

Sung Bae Park

Published by
State University of New York Press, Albany

© 2009 State University of New York

For information, contact State University of New York Press, Albany, NY
www.sunypress.edu

Production by Kelli W. LeRoux
Marketing by Anne M. Valentine

Library of Congress Cataloging-in-Publication Data

Park, Sung Bae.
    One korean's approach to buddhism : the mom/momjit paradigm /
Sung Bae Park.
        p. cm. — (Suny series in Korean studies)
    Includes bibliographical references and index.
    ISBN 978-0-7914-7697-0 (hardcover : alk. paper)
    ISBN 978-0-7914-7698-7 (pbk. : alk. paper)
    1. Spiritual life—Zen Buddhism. 2. Buddhism—Korea (South)—
Doctrines. I. Title. II. Title: Mom/momjit paradigm.

    BQ9288.P37 2009
    294.3'42—dc22   2008018857

10 9 8 7 6 5 4 3 2 1

Contents

Preface

At the very outset I would like to say that the ideas discussed on the following pages may seem repetitious at times. You may think, "The author has already said this before. Why is he saying it again?"

In response, I would like to relate the following anecdote about Confucius, the Chinese sage of the fifth century BC. He was asked by a student, "Aren't you tired of always saying the same thing over and over again?" Confucius replied, "Does the sun get tired of shining? Every morning it rises and shines all day long. It has done so since the beginning of time. Does it ever get tired?"

Similarly, you eat two or three meals every day, and have been doing so all your life. Do you ever get tired of eating? You go to sleep every night—does this ever seem repetitious? As far as life is concerned, there is always much repetition. Actually, repetition is an important part of the creative process. In terms of learning and absorbing new ideas, repetition is a crucial factor. Each time the student hears a new concept and reflects on it, his understanding deepens. It is a slow, ongoing process. So be patient—try to read with an open, nonjudgmental mind. Reflect on the ideas presented here—if at first they seem strange and unfamiliar, their repeated emphasis may help them seem less so. Hopefully, by the time you finish the book, you may find that you indeed have learned something new, or perhaps have begun to view certain things in a different light.

I also would like to offer my sincere thanks to the following people, who continually provided their unerring expertise and assistance: Hearn Chun, Yongpyo Kim, Hongkyung Kim, Robert Siegel, Biggie Ubert, and Albert Jung. I am grateful to my editorial assistant, Nancy Clough. She not only converted all my discourses into a smooth and readable written manuscript, but also provided me with invaluable guidance and suggestions concerning various controversial areas. Without her help, this book could never have been written.

Finally, I would like to express my most sincere and hearty thanks to Chin-hoe, my wife. Her consistent support and understanding have given me the strength to complete this project. To her I dedicate this book.

Introduction

I have several motivations for writing this book and would like to discuss them here in the hopes that my experiences will serve as pertinent background to the study and understanding of *mom* and *momjit*. In this way I hope to provide an easier transition into the subject for the reader whose knowledge of it may be sketchy at most.

My greatest motivation by far stems from an experience I had in the summer of 1965, an experience that directly altered the course of my life. Previous to this event, I had been employed as an assistant professor of Buddhist studies at Dongguk University in Seoul, Korea. At that time, there was a student group called the Korean Buddhist Association of University Students, within which was formed a subgroup of fifteen male students who called themselves the Seekers After Truth. I served as the advisor for this subgroup. The members were enrolled at universities near Seoul, and majored in such diverse fields as business, education, literature, philosophy, and so forth.

We decided to form our own university students' monastery, where we could live together and practice Buddhism while still attending to our academic responsibilities. We were fortunate to be allowed to stay in a nearby temple called Bong'en-sa Monastery; we lived there for about a year. The abbot of this monastery, Kwang-dŏk Sunim, became one of our two sponsors. We were given one building, which hosted a meditation hall, a lecture hall, sleeping quarters, and so forth, for our exclusive use. We were also given permission to use the temple's remaining facilities if needed. The resident monks cooked all of our meals.

Our other sponsor for this project was Mr. Han-sang Lee, who was the president of a Buddhist weekly newspaper operating out of Seoul. Mr. Lee provided us with various books and other materials as we needed them, as well as transportation between the temple and our various college campuses. He also donated money to the temple itself. Furthermore, every bit of information concerning our experience, from the beginning to the end, was written up in his newspaper and thus made known to the general public. These news items were often reported quite dramatically; I remember the first article saying something to the effect of, "This is the first student monastery ever to have existed in the 1,600-year history of Korean Buddhism." Buddhists and non-Buddhists alike became informed in this way of our every move.

During the year that we stayed at Bong'en-sa, we followed the monastery schedule at all times; the only exception to this was during the day when we had to leave the temple to attend our classes. We rose every morning at 4:00 a.m. with the monks and participated with them in the morning service, which consisted of various rituals involving bowing, chanting, and seated meditation. We then had breakfast and departed for school. At the end of the day we returned to the temple in time to have supper with the monks and to take part in the evening service, a variation of the morning's procedure. We were usually in bed by 11:00 p.m.

In the beginning, we were all very excited about our new way of life. We quickly became paragons of Buddhist practice: we were devoted and sincere, and felt extremely motivated to practice the Buddhadharma. However, we had not taken into account the limitations of our human energy systems. Our daily life was similar to that of someone who has two jobs: we had our monastery "job" as well as our school "job." It is possible for this kind of situation to succeed for awhile, but fatigue eventually builds up and becomes overwhelming, with the result that neither job is performed satisfactorily.

Our main difficulty was that we simply had no time to do our homework, write papers, or study for exams, all of which were necessary for the maintenance of our academic careers. As the quantity and quality of our academic output degenerated, everyone began to feel the strain. The only solution seemed to be to abandon the monastery schedule so that we would have the time to attend to our academic needs. Yet if this was the case, we asked ourselves, why should we continue to live in the temple at all? Furthermore, we felt that we could not back out of our commitment; as the Buddhist newspapers continued to faithfully report all of our activities, we felt that we had an ideal to uphold, both to ourselves and to the Korean community at large.

After our situation had been deteriorating in this way for a month or so, the students all began to complain. At first they discussed their problems secretly among themselves, but eventually they began to share their doubts with me. I, too, of course was experiencing the same difficulties as they. It became an increasingly agonizing set of circumstances for which no solution seemed possible.

Somehow we managed to endure these conditions for the remainder of the semester. Fortunately for us, since we had begun our monastery project in the spring, the end of that semester heralded the beginning of the summer vacation. This gave us a few months' reprieve from our academic duties, valuable time in which we hoped to find a way out of our difficulties. After some discussion we decided to embark on a journey to visit various Zen masters and seek their advice. In Korea at this time there were about twelve monks who were considered to be enlightened. Each had his own temple and most of them lived in remote mountainous areas. We decided to visit them all. The newspaper naturally reported this new development and featured an article entitled "Students Pay Visit to Zen Masters."

Much to our chagrin, our journey proved to be equally as arduous, if not more so, than our experience at the temple. For one thing, most of the Zen masters we visited had several hundred disciples, either as monks or laypersons. When they learned that we were coming, they all gathered together to await our arrival. Again, we had the uncomfortable experience of being watched. In addition to this, we were required to follow each temple's daily schedule of practice, just as we had done at Bong'en-sa. Actually we had to work even harder at these temples because we could not escape to our classes during the day. Before each Zen master received us, he would require that we first spend several days living in his temple and practicing with the other monks there. Then, after our interview with the master, we would leave the temple and board a bus that would take us to our next destination. These buses were always very crowded and we usually found ourselves having to stand for the duration of the trip, with only the straps above us to hold onto for support. We were so tired at this point that we literally fell asleep as we stood, our heads unconsciously falling to one side or the other. Occasionally one of us would accidentally jostle his neighbor, especially if the bus suddenly hit a bump in the road. Then the neighbor would wake with a start, mutter under his breath at the one who woke him, and immediately fall back to sleep. To an onlooker this may have seemed amusing, but we were in great discomfort. Needless to say, the quarreling and complaining among ourselves continued on without abating.

At last we reached our final destination, the temple of Sungchol Sunim. When we first arrived, little did we realize that our experience here would prove to be dramatically different from what occurred at the other temples. To begin with, Sungchol asked us to pay him a certain amount in tuition fees in return for our stay. When we told him we had no money, he said he did not want his payment in Korean *won*, but rather in Buddhist currency. When we asked him what he meant, he said he wanted us to prostrate three thousand times to the Buddha, that is, to the Buddhist statue in the meditation hall. We were shocked. We had thought that our fatigue was obvious. We passionately protested that we were exhausted and that there was no way that we could possibly bow three thousand times to the Buddha. Sungchol answered that if we were indeed seekers after truth, as the name of our group proclaimed, then we should be willing to follow the seeker's way of life, even if it meant our own death. He told us in no uncertain terms that if we were unwilling to do as he asked, we would have to leave the temple. He added, however, that he knew we were able to carry out his request, otherwise he would not have made such a request in the first place. He inquired whether we thought he was stupid, asking us to do something which he knew we could not do. He said that if that were case, then we should leave immediately, but then reiterated that he knew we could do what he was asking.

Somehow, I think primarily due to his faith in us, we were finally persuaded to give it a try. However, at this point, as soon as we had agreed to make the effort to perform the bows, Sungchol warned us that we would not be allowed to stop in the middle, adding that if we felt we could not perform all three thousand prostrations, then we should not even bother to begin them. He thus probed our degree of determination, making sure to emphasize the importance of our full commitment to the task at hand. We all said that we would definitely be able to complete the full program of three thousand prostrations.

The day of July 31, 1965, dawned hot and sticky; it turned out to be one of the hottest days of the year. That date is clearly etched in my mind. Thirteen of us solemnly entered the Buddha hall that morning; it felt as if we were entering a sauna. There were no windows, no air conditioner, not even a fan, and the bare wood floor did nothing to ease the impact of our bodies coming into contact with it over and over again in seemingly endless succession. Furthermore, we were not permitted to leave the meditation hall at any time for any reason, not even to drink a glass of water or to use the bathroom. Various monks took turns beating the rhythm of our movements with a drum and performing a ritual involving incense sticks to count out the number of prostrations as we performed them.

We all began to move in unison. After the first hundred prostrations, we were truly exhausted. After three hundred, we realized that what we were attempting was impossible, yet somehow we kept going. Sometimes one of us would stay down on the floor in the middle of a prostration, and refuse to get up. However, soon his neighbor would haul him back up to a standing position, exhorting him to keep moving. The last five hundred bows were the worst. I don't know how we managed to keep on going. Yet somehow, thirteen hours after we had begun, we were amazed to realize that every single one of us had performed his final three thousandth prostration! However, I must admit that during those thirteen hours, there were few of us who did not resist criticizing, if not out-and-out condemning wholeheartedly, the entire religion of Buddhism, including all the Zen masters who practiced it!

Then, to our utter disbelief, we found that Sungchol had one more surprise in store for us. He asked us to climb the mountain behind the monastery. Although you, the reader, may now be groaning in empathy at the seeming cruelty of this request, I actually felt that it was not a bad idea, as it would enable us as to stretch our muscles in a new way, which they greatly needed to do after being restricted to performing just one up and down motion for so many hours. And the truth was, we all felt like heroes at this point; we ended up gleefully undertaking the climb, sometimes even shouting for joy as we walked.

When we returned, bone-tired but radiant, we were at last granted an interview with Sungchol. He asked us what we had come for and we explained our dilemma. He then responded with a discourse that significantly altered both the course of my philosophical and religious studies as well as my entire life. He told us that our problem was simple. "You are attached to *momjit*," he proclaimed. Now every Korean has heard of the terms *mom* and *momjit* since childhood. They are words with very ancient origins and may be here translated as "essence" (*mom*) and "function" (*momjit*). Yet in all the years that I had studied Buddhism, I had never before heard these words used in a Buddhist context.

At this point, I would like to interrupt my story in order to describe the pedagogical principle we were attempting to follow at our student monastery. We had chosen Samantabhadra Bodhisattva as our model for practice. This important bodhisattva of Mahāyāna Buddhism is associated with a well-known text entitled "The Ten Vows of Samantabhadra Bodhisattva."[1] This text exists as the last chapter of the Avatamsaka Sūtra, a noted work of the Hua-yen school of Buddhism. This sect, founded in China, teaches the equality of all things and the dependence of all things on one another. It was due to our enormous respect and appreciation for this text that we organized our little group in the first place, and then made our plans to stay at Bong'en-sa.

According to Sungchol, the ten vows of Samantabhadra Bodhisattva represent the realm of *momjit*, or his natural way of functioning; therefore, making these vows came very naturally to him. However, Sungchol told us, you are not Samantabhadra Bodhisattva, and no matter how hard you try to imitate his world of *momjit*, you cannot succeed. What you must do, he said, is to transform your *mom*, your own essence; you must in effect transform your own *mom* to that of Samantabhadra Bodhisattva. If you can do this, then you will have no problem, for then your *momjit* will be the same as his. Without such a transformation, you are merely imitating the behavior of a great bodhisattva.

Sungchol then reminded us of an old Korean proverb, which states, "A sparrow cannot win a race if he is competing with a crane." This is because the crane's long legs will easily outdistance the sparrow with its short little legs. Sungchol told us that our *momjit* was that of the sparrow, yet we were attempting to imitate the *momjit* of the crane. If we pursued in such an endeavor, he warned, our legs would break.

It was at this point that I realized my mistake. I have learned many things from the Buddha and bodhisattvas, yet up until this point I had always viewed them from a *momjit* perspective, that is, their functions and operations as human beings, and had tried to imitate them as such. This had provided the basis for my system of philosophical and religious inquiry. I had never really attempted to incorporate their *mom* into myself, transforming it into my own *mom*. Sungchol truly opened my eyes to the error of such a position.

As a result of this experience, I resigned from my position at Dongguk University and became a monk at Sungchol's temple for a number of years. Ever since that day in 1965 I have been examining myself unceasingly, asking, "What are you doing? Are you merely imitating the *momjit*, the external appearance?" There is a qualitative difference between the act of seeing into one's fundamental structure and that of merely imitating appearances. The former brings one into contact with his own *mom*, whereas the latter is just following along in the realm of *momjit* and will not produce any deep, long-lasting results.

Sungchol's sermon had the effect of a deep shock, waking me up from what I viewed as my bitter failure both at Bong'en-sa and at the other Zen masters' temples (before our visit to Sungchol). Most people tend to view the spiritual life in terms of their own fantasies and dreams, perceiving spiritual practitioners as utterly tranquil, devoted, and selfless. I knew from my own experience that this was not the case; people who pursue a spiritual way of life are normal human beings, possessing the same hopes and fears and suffering the same disappointments as anyone else. When Sungchol delivered his earth-shattering (at least, to my ears) sermon on that hot summer day in 1965, it served to awaken me to a deeper understanding of the real meaning of spirituality.

I stayed at Sungchol's monastery, Haein-sa, for a period of about three years, studying and practicing under his tutelage. By the way, this monastery still exists today. Now, however, it has spread out into various locations, in which approximately five hundred monks and nuns live and practice together.

Returning to lay life, however, after my three-year monastic experience served as another kind of shock for me. I quickly realized that there now existed quite a large gap between my inner world and the world that surrounded me. I saw that my philosophical understanding had been strongly influenced by the *mom*-oriented culture of the monastery. I perceived over and over again, at almost every moment of contact with the outer world, that people were not in touch with this *mom* realm, but rather lived their lives primarily within the tenacious yet all-pervading confines of the *momjit* sphere of activity. I myself had no interest whatsoever in seeking a reputation or making a lot of money, for I saw that those things were impermanent and thus illusory. It dawned on me that my entire value system had undergone a complete and radical transformation. Before becoming a monk, even though I had considered myself a Buddhist, I still saw myself as a participating member in the world of *momjit*. My stay in the monastery, however, had significantly altered my karmic direction. Although I was not aware of these inner changes while they were occurring, after I left the monastery it became increasingly obvious to me that I had become a completely different person.

All the great sages of Korea, both Confucian and Buddhist, have been deeply aware of the distinction between *mom* and *momjit*. Each in his own way has striven to impart the primary value of *mom* to his disciples and students. After I had experienced a *mom*-oriented way of life for myself, I truly appreciated for the first time the crucial point these sages were trying to convey. I believe that the crux of their message is this: in order to operate freely, *mom* cannot be forced or interfered with, nor can it be produced by the manipulation of *momjit*. Many people attempt to imitate a spiritual leader's deeds or actions (his *momjit*) in the hopes of attaining what he has attained. This is a self-defeating task. To try to produce an effect based on one's own limited understanding or desires will never yield the hoped-for results.

Rather, what is needed is to allow *mom* to operate on its own, in its own way and in its own time. Only then, when the conditions are right, will the desired effect automatically spring forth.

I stated above that ordinary people (as opposed to monks and nuns) live in a *momjit* culture. Yet the majority of these people, at least in East Asian society, although not sages themselves, possess at least some understanding and appreciation of the value of *mom*. Furthermore, although this may no longer be the case, when I was growing up in rural Korea about sixty years ago, the goal of every Korean parent was for his or her child to become a Confucian sage. This was certainly the case in my own family. By this time, Korea had been heavily influenced by the teachings of Confucianism for many hundreds of years, and a Confucian education was considered to be of primary importance. The purpose of such an education, as I said, was to make the child a sage, who may here be defined as a person who values *mom* over *momjit* and lives his life accordingly.

Before my monastery experience, I had been unable to fully appreciate this principle of education, which had been so diligently pursued by my parents. Throughout my childhood my father had constantly urged me to act like a "great man" (Chinese: *da ren*), the paragon of Confucian sagehood. Yet although what he was saying seemed to ring true, I cannot say that I really made any strong efforts to achieve such a goal for myself. I think that this is probably true in most households and within the educational system as well. People may respect what their parents are trying to convey to them, yet they are unable to deeply appreciate or respond to their words on a fundamental level. Their respect tends to remain rather superficial, as it is based on an intellectual understanding rather than being a gut-level realization stemming from their own experience. My own case is certainly no exception.

When I returned to lay society, however, and became cognizant of the many disparities between things, disparities that I had never seen before, I realized that there existed a strong similarity between my parents' principle of education and that of the sages. Although my parents never used the word *mom*, its underlying message was continuously present in whatever they attempted to teach me. I saw that although the effect of their teaching was hidden, it ran like a steady undercurrent throughout my life. I had not realized this before. Yet again, I saw with sadness that although others respected the value of *mom*, both within their home and out in the world, they were not able to make use of it as the fundamental motivating force in their lives. They paid it a certain lip service, so to speak, yet continued to allow the influences of *momjit* to rule their every thought, word, and deed.

When I came with my wife and children to the United States in 1969, I received yet another shock. At first, of course, every new experience was quite fascinating. There were many new discoveries to be made, and the rapid pace of life gave the very air I breathed a sense of constant excitement and expectation. For the first time in my life I had a car, a TV, and a home of my own.

Just like a honeymoon, however, the high eventually began to wear off. As if out of a cocoon, my internal karma began to emerge, and I started to painfully experience the enormous disparity between American and Asian culture. The media continually kept me informed of the various problems that exist in this country, and I encountered various personal difficulties as well. Everything around me differed radically from what I had been accustomed to: the language, customs, ways of thinking, behavior, style of living—everything. The all-pervading influence of *momjit* was glaringly apparent. I saw all too clearly that Asian culture, though lacking a full or deep appreciation of *mom*, as I said before, still maintains a far greater awareness of its existence than the culture of the West.

This fact has a subtle but crucial significance. In a *mom*-oriented world, every visible object or entity has an invisible aspect to it. For example, when someone says, "I love you," or "I hate you," there are other factors that are operating aside from the obvious message of the words themselves. One who lives from a *mom*-based perspective will be deeply aware of this. The essential value of the *mom/momjit* paradigm is that these two aspects, the invisible and the visible, are interdependent; one cannot exist without the other. *Mom* itself lies inherent within every occurrence of *momjit*, just as *momjit* does not dwell apart from *mom*. Yet due to our misunderstanding of the nature of their relationship, we are unable to perceive the one as it exists within the other and thus we tend to see only the one or the other. Our deepest inclination is to separate them off from each other. This is due in part to the nature of language itself, which lacks the capacity to view two things simultaneously. The mind, too, lacks this ability. A *mom*-based culture, however, is able to recognize the inherent existence of the one within the other, and a person who lives in such a culture will obviously have access to a much deeper understanding of his own life, the lives of those he comes in contact with, and the nature of life itself.

My final motivation for writing this book concerns the realm of academics. Most of my scholarly work has involved interpreting and commenting on the classical texts of Confucianism, Buddhism, and Taoism. During the course of my academic studies I have discovered that many scholars in the West have not always correctly understood or interpreted these classics. This is due in part, I believe, to their lack of familiarity with the *mom/momjit* paradigm. For example, in the well-known Platform Sūtra, the monk Hui-neng often uses the term *wu-nien*. Now, although *wu* can be translated as "no" or "not" and *nien* means "thinking" or "thought," to translate *wu-nien* as "no thinking" or "no thought" is incorrect. Why is this so? "No" here does not indicate nonexistence, as reflected by the words *void* or *emptiness*; rather, it is used as a negation of the dualism with which we normally perceive things. Thus, *wu* or "no" here refers to no differences between things, that is, no differentiation between subject and object, good and evil, and so forth. The message of *wu-nien* is that to obtain the *wu* or "no" of dualism is to automatically align oneself with Buddha's thought. Thus, *wu-nien* = no dualistic thought = Buddha's thought. Yet although *wu-nien* does not mean that one should stop thinking or have no thoughts, this seems to be how Westerners often view this term. In terms of *mom* and *momjit*, "no" here means "no *momjit*," thus resulting in freedom from the dualism of the *momjit* orientation. Once one is freed from *momjit*, *mom* naturally flows forth unimpeded. To focus on *momjit* as a means to achieve the end result of *mom* is to force the issue, so to speak. Only when one can free himself from this compulsion can the *mom* manifest itself. This subtle understanding, I feel, is crucial if scholars are to successfully interpret the classical works of East Asia.

In conclusion, I would like to reiterate that in a *mom*-oriented culture, education, and especially self-education, is primary. What is esteemed above all, as mentioned earlier, is the making of a "great man," that is, one who willingly seeks to be of service to others rather than seeking his own personal profit at their expense. In order to do this, he must be familiar with his own inner workings. Fundamentally, he must be able to make the distinction between his attachment to *momjit*, the external appearance, and his return to *mom*, which ceaselessly and freely flows within him. In the next chapters I will discuss these ideas in more detail in the hopes that a deeper understanding of this vital model of thought may be made accessible to a wider audience.

Please note that I have used the pronoun "he" to refer to any person of either gender; although I did not use the cumbersome "he/she," I did not intend to exclude the female gender from the meaning of the particular passage.

CHAPTER ONE

Initial Considerations

SOCIOLOGICAL CONCERNS

As I mentioned in the introduction, the terms *mom* and *momjit* are familiar to all Koreans, and have their roots in ancient history. Although I translated them in the introduction as "essence" and "function," a more accurate definition (and the one the Korean populace is more familiar with) is "body" and "the body's functions." The implications of "essence/function" and "body/its functions" are similar, that is, both paradigms are used to point to a nondual relationship between the two concepts. There is a subtle but crucial difference, however, between the two models, "essence/function" and "body/its functions." The term *essence/function* (which is often translated by East Asian scholars into the Chinese term *t'i-yung*) has a rather abstract, philosophical tone, connoting an impression of being somewhat removed from the nitty-gritty details of everyday life. My primary interest, however, is in the human being's personal understanding and experience of nonduality. How are we able to access this nondual realm? It is only through our practice. What, then, is practice? It lies right within all the events that make up our ordinary, everyday lives. Practice occurs within our own bodies, which in turn are the breeding ground for many types of functions, such as consciousness, emotions, thoughts, beliefs, value systems, and so forth. Practice is the overall context within which all these various functions, or processes, are operating—right here and right now.

The terms *mom* and *momjit*, then, far from being removed from our daily lives, help us return back to our bodies, our most basic significators of what we experience on a day-to-day basis. Our bodies are performing their various functions at every moment. There is no way we can avoid experiencing these functions. These terms *mom* and *momjit* are priceless tools pointing to the nondual reality that exists within us at this very moment.

11

Within the field of cross-cultural studies, it is generally agreed that Asian cultures are *mom*-oriented, whereas the West is strongly influenced by *momjit*. It can also be said that traditional cultures of the past were by and large based on *mom*, while contemporary societies, whether Eastern or Western, clearly have a *momjit* bias. It should be noted that although Asian culture has its roots in a *mom* way of life, due to the influence of Western technology the Asian lifestyle is increasingly becoming more and more *momjit*-based. It is important to keep in mind, however, that *mom* and *momjit* should not be viewed as separate aspects, as they are essentially intertwined and interdependent. Yet the intriguing paradox of the paradigm is this: although each aspect cannot exist apart from the other, it maintains an identity of its own. Furthermore, within any given culture the identity of one or the other will be clearly predominant. Thus, in order to have a proper understanding of the model in its entirety we need to differentiate between the two parts which form its structure.

In traditional Asian society, the role of the individual was seen as crucial to the well-being of the society. If any one person neglected his responsibilities either to himself or to the world around him, he was not considered worthy of the respect of others. In matters of spiritual training in particular, it was understood that any individual's weaknesses or deficiencies needed to be addressed and corrected through his own efforts. This naturally required an understanding on his part of the proper use of his mind.

In our capitalistic, industrialized world, however, the individual is continually discouraged from making such use of his mental capacities. He is instead urged to follow the rules strictly as laid out by the social norms; as a result, the individual is becoming more and more like a machine. There is becoming less and less room for him to maneuver around in, and less and less space for him to listen to the dictates of his own consciousness. He is instead encouraged to expend all of his efforts in conforming to his society's various requirements and conditions. If he adapts to these requirements, he is considered a success; his own inner state is given little, if any, consideration.

INDIVIDUAL NEEDS

In our modern world, then, with its busyness and its "progressive" aspirations, the conscientiousness of the individual is rated very low on the scale of values. He is constantly being prodded, like a sheep in a flock, to respond to the influences of the extended world, *momjit*, at the continuous expense of his own internal needs and values, *mom*. Even religious leaders often fall prey to this insidious and devastating imbalance of the natural order.

This does not mean, of course, that an inner realm does not exist within each one of us. We all have very active internal lives, yet often our experience of our own inner world causes us enormous suffering. What does it mean that an increasing number of people are seeking the aid of psychologists and psychiatrists in order to manage their lives? This fact, I believe, points to our inability to reconcile our own inner *mom* world with the *momjit* world, which exists outside of us. We insist on creating a separation between the two where none exists. We split *momjit* off from *mom* and then proceed to spend most of our time and energy catering to the distorted *momjit* we have created. For example, following our parents' teaching, we tell our children that they must always try to look happy in front of others, that they should smile, and say the right thing, and so forth. This manifestation of *momjit* represents a distortion of *mom* and prevents its natural expression, causing us deep, often unconscious, inner distress.

Such suffering, caused by the contradictions we make between our internal needs and the requirements of our society, must eventually seek an outlet, a means of escape. This will often occur on an unconscious level. Minor ways in which we may attempt to escape may be through forgetfulness or perhaps changing the subject of conversation. Other methods may be more radical, such as taking drugs or quitting one's job. None of these tactics, however, will solve the problem, for it exists inherently within us.

The teachings of Buddhism tell us that we must confront our suffering; we must face it and see it as it is, rather than attempt to escape from it. According to the Buddha, we cause our own suffering, through our attachments. We hear about something, or see something, and then we want to hold onto it as if it is a permanent entity that exists within a fixed time and place. It is our six sense organs (the mind being the sixth) that perceive these objects or entities, and thus they are the most obvious and immediate causes of our attachment. Yet if we look deeper, we will discern the deep desire that underlies all of our clinging. We are drawn to someone, to something, or to an idea because it appeals to us, and then we want to take possession of it and give it a permanent place in our lives. If our desire for these things did not exist, they would merely be like birds in the sky: they would appear before us for awhile and then they would eventually disappear.

HUMAN IGNORANCE

As we investigate further into our attachment, and seek its deepest origins, we may see that it is ultimately a product of our ignorance (Sanskrit: *avidyā*). Essentially, we may come to realize that all of our perceptions, desires, aversions, and so forth, are caused by a false idea of the self. We view our physical body as our self and we see it as permanent, just as we see physical objects, people, and ideas as permanent. Yet according to Buddhist teachings, the self is merely part of an ongoing process of creation and destruction, which Buddhism calls dependent origination (Sanskrit: *pratītya samutpāda*). The self is—and we are—only one link in a vast universal chain of interconnectedness and interdependence. None of us exists outside of this intricate, all-encompassing web, and therefore none of us can escape the cycle of death and rebirth. We are not permanent entities, firmly fixed at this particular place and time; rather we, just like every atom of existence, are participants in an eternal process of change.

Our suffering, then, whether we live in the East or West, in ancient times or modern, originates from our misguided attachment to that which is impermanent. All manifestations of *momjit*, whether they be objects or people or feelings or ideas, are themselves impermanent. By its very nature, *momjit* can only be temporary, yet in our ignorance as to the real nature of things we view it—and hold onto it—as eternal. Although a part of us is aware that *momjit* is impermanent—for example, we all know that one day we will die—we constantly emphasize and exaggerate its value. This helps to give it a greater sense of solidarity and enables us to fool ourselves into thinking that it will endure forever. Enlightened Zen masters tell us that if we can eliminate our attachment to the idea of an eternal *momjit*, we will be liberated, that is, released from all our suffering, and experience lasting peace, freedom, and joy. These qualities depict the realm of *mom*, which is utterly free from any attachment whatsoever. When attachment arises, then, it signifies the presence of *momjit*; when the attachment is eliminated, *mom* manifests spontaneously.

What exactly is *mom*? Although we have seen that *momjit* can be defined as fragmentary and partial, and capable of being fixed in time and place, *mom* cannot be placed within the confines of any description whatsoever. The closest we can come to describing *mom* is as a negation of *momjit*. Thus, for example, *nirvāṇa* (whose meaning is similar to *mom*) is referred to as neither arising nor ceasing. In this context, even birth and death are considered examples of *momjit*, whereas *mom*, in comparison, may be seen as universality itself. This will be discussed in greater detail in a later section.

ORDINARY AND ABSOLUTE ASPECTS

It is important to understand that *mom* and *momjit* may refer to either one of two radically different strata of reality and/or awareness: the ordinary and the absolute (the latter may also be called the religious). One way to view the ordinary level is to see it as pertaining to our mundane, everyday life. Another perspective involves viewing the ordinary level as the application of the absolute or religious level to our daily existence and activities. This latter approach helps to imbue our daily routine with a deeper significance, which may be of great value to those who are attempting to pursue a more spiritual way of life. However we view it, an understanding of the ordinary level is crucial in terms of our communication with others, for it is obvious that it is at this level, namely, the ordinary, that we perform all of our day-to-day activities and conduct all our relationships.

One of the simplest ways of understanding *mom* and *momjit* on the ordinary level is through the metaphor of a tree. Although I am not sure of its origins, this metaphor is an extremely apt model for our purposes here. A tree consists of roots, a trunk, branches, leaves, and perhaps flowers or fruit. If we consider the roots, or the hidden part, to correspond to *mom*, and the remainder of the tree, that is, the trunk, branches, leaves, and flowers/fruit, which are all visible, to be *momjit*, then we may have a clear idea not only of the identity of *mom* and *momjit*, but also of their relationship to each other. Thus, we may see that in this context *mom* is primarily the hidden, invisible aspect of an entity and yet one that provides support and nourishment for the rest of it. Correspondingly, *momjit* represents the external, visible part, that which performs various functions throughout the course of the life of the entity. It should also be clear through the use of this metaphor that the two aspects, whether they be *mom* and *momjit*, roots and branches, or foundation and function, are interdependent. If one were somehow separated from the other, neither one would be able to continue to exist. In the case of the tree, if the roots (*mom*) are cut off or neglected, the tree will die, and thus its function, or *momjit*, will also be denied. Similarly, the roots (*mom*) can never just exist by themselves but will eventually, with care and nurturing, be a springboard for the creation and growth of the rest of the tree (*momjit*). Applied to the life of a human being, we may see that, for example, if a person experiences a deep emotion of some sort (*mom*), whether it be love or hate or fear or whatever, it must of necessity find a way of expressing itself through the words or actions of that person's life (*momjit*). If that same emotion is not able to manifest itself outwardly in the person's life, it will eventually cause him much pain and even damage. On the other hand, from the perspective of *momjit*, whatever action (*momjit*) a person undertakes is never random but is rather directly connected to some inner belief or value (*mom*) that he holds.

The insight the tree metaphor offers us is twofold. First, it helps us to understand that to place a priority on the external aspect at the expense of the internal is a grave mistake, for the internal always holds the position of higher value. You can chop off the branches of a tree if you wish, and you can even chop down the trunk, but in time, if the roots are healthy and receive the correct care, the tree will grow back. However, if you wish for the tree to grow you can never destroy the roots; it simply cannot exist without them. Similarly, in the life of a human being, if one merely pays attention to external appearances without nourishing his own inner needs and values, it is extremely doubtful that he will be able to find lasting happiness or peace. By discovering and nurturing his roots, however, or his inner sense of identity, he may create a firm foundation which will serve as an anchor to protect him from any outer difficulty he may encounter.

This understanding of the value of the internal over the external leads us directly to the second insight offered by the tree metaphor. This insight is essentially a variation or an expansion of the first: if you wish to correct any mistake, strengthen any weakness, and create and develop a strong, solid life (*momjit*), you must discover and return to the root itself (*mom*); you will not be able to achieve your goals without doing so. This truth is well illustrated by a story that appears in the book of Mencius, an extremely influential Confucian thinker of ancient China. In this story, a certain farmer went out to his rice fields one morning to see how his rice plants were doing. When he discovered that some plants were shorter than others, he interpreted this to mean that they were not as healthy, and he proceeded to pull on them in an attempt to make them taller. Later, he went back home to tell his family of his wonderful deed. When the whole family returned to the field the next day to check on the progress of the plants, they discovered to their dismay that every single one had perished overnight.

Even to those of us who have been born and raised in the city, the mistake of the farmer seems obvious. Yet the lesson the story intends to convey is significant: by paying attention only to the external appearance of the rice plant, he sacrificed the life of the entire plant. If he had been able to view the plant in its entirety, he would have realized that in order to make it grow taller, its roots were what needed strengthening. To attempt a cure through means of the stalk was totally ineffectual—worse, it killed the plant.

The kind of care and attention needed here, that is, the nurturing of the root, is an act that cannot be completed in a day or a week. It requires much time and diligent effort. The tree has a certain principle of growth: it needs water, good soil, sunshine, and so forth. These different elements all must be recognized and valued. This same understanding may be applied to human relationships and activities as well. We need to look into our relationships and our activities more deeply. What is the root? And what are the branches, the leaves, the flowers? In my view, to care for others covertly, rather than in a direct way, may be seen as the root of a relationship. To help someone in an immediate, obvious sense will often be viewed by him with suspicion, but if you perform a service for him without his knowledge, then you are truly giving him something of value. The results may not be instantaneous, but they will eventually become known and will then produce a situation of benefit to all concerned.

In a similar vein, let us look at the example of two people meeting, whether for the first time or on a regular basis, on either a social or professional level. The meeting itself may seem like a very powerful event, as the two people are interacting with each other directly, on an immediate level of experience. This meeting, the external event itself, may be termed as *momjit*. However, what about what happens behind the scenes, after the meeting is over? Doesn't that have the greater impact? That is when each participant is afforded the time and space in which to mull over the events that occurred earlier, and to formulate his views accordingly. The interval that occurs after the meeting, then, may be termed *mom*, and it may be seen to possess the greater significance, the more long-lasting influence.

I would like to relate here a personal experience, which I feel reflects this understanding very well. When I first came to Stony Brook as an assistant professor in 1979, my field of Buddhism was placed as a subdivision within a larger academic field, the department of comparative studies. At one point during my first semester of teaching, the chairman of the department accused me of appropriating some funds which he felt had been earmarked for his own use. He stormed into my office one day and berated me vehemently for "stealing" his funds. In fact, these funds had been allocated to me so that I could set up a scholarship for some students in Korea. After he made his accusation, I felt I had no choice but to seek the aid of a higher authority, the dean of the department, for guidance. After hearing what happened, the dean wrote a letter to the chairman informing him that he (the dean) had indeed designated that the money be set aside for my use in helping some students from my country. After he received this letter, the chairman's attitude toward me changed completely, and he began to treat me with warmth and cordiality. I felt uncomfortable, however, as I did not know the nature of his true feelings toward me. I decided to see what I could do to be of service to him, yet as I did not wish to cause him any embarrassment or discomfort, I made sure that none of my actions was overt or obvious. Instead, just like a parent who silently helps his children in numberless ways, I began to perform a few minor, unobtrusive tasks in order to make his life run a little more smoothly. Later, these small efforts had a very large impact on both our relationship and my career. Indeed, when the matter of my tenure came up for approval, the chairman's was one of the strongest voices in favor of my promotion.

This story well exemplifies, I believe, the inestimable value of *mom*. It acts unobtrusively yet persistently, and affects *momjit* in ways that cannot be directly or immediately perceived. Both of the references mentioned above, the metaphor of the tree and the story of the farmer, aptly point to the value of *mom* in relation to *momjit* and invite us to apply the implications of such a relationship to our own lives.

However, the drawback to these references is that neither one accounts for the religious aspect of the paradigm, that is, the aspect of nonduality. In recognition of this aspect, it may be said that even in an unhealthy branch or leaf of a tree, and even in the farmer's dying rice plants, *mom* can be found to exist. Although these metaphors and stories are not concerned with such a truth, the truth is there if one looks deeply enough into the matter. *Mom* exists in everything and everyone, whether healthy or unhealthy, visible or invisible, rich or poor, smart or stupid. There is not one atom in the universe that does not contain *mom*, nor is there one thought or perception in which it is lacking.

Thus, within a family, for example, *mom* may be seen to represent the respect shown by one member of the family to another. If one family member becomes ill, he must be tended to by another or others, no matter what his position within the family structure, until the other regains his health. I am the youngest in a family of eight children, having two older sisters and five older brothers. When I went to Korea in 1997, I paid a visit to my oldest sister, who is now eighty-five years old. She was having some trouble with her teeth and required extensive dental work. When I went to see her, she asked me, "I am so old now. Do I really need to go to a dentist and have this work done?" I told her, "Even if you know you are going to die tomorrow, you should go see a dentist today. It is very important to always do whatever needs to be done."

The German philosopher Immanuel Kant said that the human being should not be treated as the means to an end, but as the end itself, that is, as the subject of one's awareness. The human being is not merely an outward manifestation of some mystical essence, but is the essence himself; he contains everything with himself, worlds within worlds. Even if he is sick, old, deteriorating, a criminal, stupid, clumsy, or whatever, he should not be treated merely as a means for achieving some future purpose. He is one link which connects to another in the ongoing process of the creation and development of the universe. This is what is meant by the Buddhist term "dependent origination."

As we said before, *mom* has two meanings. It is not only a part of the whole, or one side of a coin, which is its ordinary meaning or aspect, but it is also the whole coin itself, front and back. This latter is its religious aspect. It is important to remember here that this whole cannot be perceived through the five sense organs (or six, if you include the mind), just as you cannot see both sides of the coin at the same time. If you are attached to the sense organs as a means by which to identify something or make a judgment about it, you will never understand it in its entirety, its *mom*. Within this religious aspect, *mom* cannot be identified or expressed or described.

All of the various Buddhist terms, such as emptiness, suchness, *nirvāṇa*, enlightenment, and so forth, have the capacity to be structured within a system corresponding to that of *mom* and *momjit*. For example, when discussing Buddha-nature, which in this context may be equated with *mom*, the material, temporal aspect of Buddha-nature (its *momjit*) needs to be recognized and included. Although it is believed to exist in opposition to one's Buddha-nature, we have seen that this is not really the case, as opposition implies duality, whereas the relationship of *mom* to *momjit* is of a nondual nature.

People often tend to make the mistake of believing that *mom* is always an invisible aspect. As we pointed out earlier, this is not always the case; the determining factor must always be the context within which the issue is being discussed or investigated. For example, we may say that a pen is *mom*, that is, a visible aspect. However, its function, which is the writing, is *momjit*. On the other hand, we could also say that the desire to write represents *mom*; in this case the pen now becomes *momjit*, as it is the implement needed to perform the function of writing.

Following this line of thought, *momjit* is often believed to be visible, yet again, this is not always so. We may say that the mental or emotional aspects of one's life, even though invisible, are *momjit*, for they represent the function or manifestation of one's deeper identity, his *mom*. Compared to one's actions, however, thoughts or emotions are the *mom*, the motivating force, and the actions themselves, existing as the manifestation or function of the thoughts and emotions, become the *momjit*. Similarly, take the example of one person offering service to another, which is a type of function and thus represents *momjit*. A visible manifestation of this would be his driving a sick person to the doctor, whereas the invisible aspect might be the prayers that he makes for that same person, or perhaps just his general feelings of concern. Whether visible or invisible, however, all manifestations of *momjit* may be defined as impermanent.

The *mom/momjit* paradigm originated as a means to help human beings deal with the fundamental problem of suffering. It is a device that was intended to be used to investigate this problem at a deeper level than is ordinarily possible. The terms *mom* and *momjit* were not created apart from this purpose. This is an important point. If one attempts to formulate a definition or description of these two terms on an abstract level, in isolation from the larger philosophical and religious issues concerning human existence, he will run into difficulties.

What, then, is the correlation between *mom* and *momjit* on the one hand and human existence on the other? We have seen that from a religious perspective, everything that is not-me is related to me; I am a part, however infinitesimal, of every speck of existence in the universe. Similarly, there is no *momjit* that does not contain *mom*. *Mom* is everywhere.

The value of a simile or metaphor is that once its meaning has been understood, it must be abandoned, for it is no longer necessary. Its only purpose is as a tool for understanding. The Diamond Sūtra, a landmark text of Mahāyāna Buddhism, utilizes the metaphor of a raft that takes one to the shore across the river. When one reaches the other shore, he must abandon the raft, for it has served its purpose and is not needed anymore. Another metaphor used quite often by East Asian Buddhists is that of a finger that points to the moon. In this case the moon refers to the experience of enlightenment, whereas the finger represents any device used to bring one to, or to "point" to, that experience. The message is similar to that of the raft: once enlightenment is realized, the finger is no longer needed. Its mission has been accomplished.

Mom and *momjit* must be approached in the same way. They help point the way to a deeper understanding of human existence; once that understanding has been reached they should not be clung to as independent isolated entities in themselves.

SUFFERING

I am in agreement with the Buddha that even in the midst of all of our technological achievements and material comforts, the crux of the human condition is its fundamental suffering. Surely, there is no one on this earth who does not experience some level of dissatisfaction with his life. The Buddha delineated a fourfold list of sufferings, which included birth, sickness, old age, and death. He also mentioned the suffering caused by attachment to what is pleasant and aversion for the unpleasant. In my view, the majority of our suffering is caused by the great discrepancy we have created between our inner world of thoughts and feelings and the world outside of us, the world of human relationships. This discrepancy is usually the result of our self-deceit, which may be translated as our inability or unwillingness to view these two realms, the inner and the outer, clearly. Why do we suffer so much in this way? I believe it is due to the fact that we adhere to a value system that derives from a utilitarian approach to life, in which our actions are motivated by the primary purpose of achieving benefit for ourselves in some way or another. These benefits, whatever their nature, are all directly related to the world of *momjit*. Yet as we have previously discussed, *momjit* cannot survive without the presence of *mom*. Because of our attachment we cannot see this; therefore, it is only by detaching ourselves on all levels—intellectually, emotionally, and sensually—from *momjit*, that we may apprehend the *mom* inherent within these desires. Only in this way may our suffering be overcome.

DEFINITION OF *MOM* AND *MOMJIT*: A CLOSER LOOK

How can we describe *mom*? Words cannot accomplish this. Perhaps the closest we can come is to say that *mom* is what enables *momjit* to exist. The definition of *momjit* is more accessible; it is whatever can be expressed, described, or defined, and is by nature temporal, momentary, and impermanent. With my hand, I am able to grasp and then release various objects. These objects, as well as my hand, belong to the realm of *momjit*. What is *mom* in this example? It is what causes my hand to grasp and release. One may say, "Oh, well, then, *mom* is the signal given to the hand by the brain." But the brain is not *mom*; it is *momjit*. What is it that gives the signal to the brain to open or close the hand?

The nature of any discussion about *mom* within the visible world, that is, in the ordinary aspect, will be utilitarian. The invisible aspect of *mom*, however, points to a soteriological concern, and in this context *mom* may be said to be universal and eternal. How is it possible for *mom* to have this added religious dimension? People normally do not have difficulty in understanding *mom* in its visible aspect—as the body, for example. To comprehend its religious dimension, however, presents a bigger problem for many.

Perhaps at this point we should discuss what is meant by the religious dimension. What does the word *religion* mean? Religions may be labeled Eastern or Western and will accordingly differ in many ways. In what sense, then, is something considered to be religious? A Buddhist might say that the religious aspect of something allows for the simultaneous existence of two fundamentally different or opposing conditions. It is in this way that we may begin to comprehend the religious dimension of *mom*. In this context *mom* is both individual, that is, partial and impermanent, as well as universal or eternal. Thus, its religious, or universal, aspect includes the ordinary or temporal. It should be clear here that *mom* embraces and includes *momjit* as well. This religious aspect may be equated with the Buddhist term *emptiness*. This emptiness does not mean the same thing as nothingness, however, but is rather an all-embracing completeness, which is empty only in the sense that it possesses no inherent identity of its own. As asserted by the Buddhist doctrine of dependent origination, within the religious aspect of *mom* each atom of existence is seen to arise within the context of another such atom, and ceases within the same context. Thus, it does not arise and cease of its own volition, as an isolated, independent, abstract entity, but is instead directly related to and dependent upon all other entities in the universe for its existence. Furthermore, it contains every other atom of the universe within it as well. In Hua-yen literature, which we will investigate in a later chapter, each atom of existence, each speck of dust, is said to contain the entire universe. Indeed, it *is* the entire universe. Similarly, the smallest unit of time (Sanskrit: *kshana*) may be considered in the same way. It contains all time within it: past, present, and future.

This is the mysterious aspect of Buddhism, according to Western scholars. This word *mysterious*, however, is misleading. In the West, it usually refers to something that has no logic, and is seen as superstitious or mystical. For followers of Buddhist thought, however, this awareness of the universality of time and space is not seen as a mystical or mysterious concept, although it does contain that aspect. If one accepts the truth of this awareness, everyone is seen as a Buddha and everyone and everything has value; nothing is useless. Furthermore, each moment, each action, each thought and word, has equal value, for each contains the entire universe within it. The opening of a flower in spring is the same as its wilting in autumn. Each thing includes all others. *Mom* and *momjit*, too, are contained within each other: neither stands by itself.

THE EXPERIENCE OF *MOM*

Although *mom* cannot be adequately described or defined, it can be experienced, and once its meaning is ascertained, then *momjit* will easily be understood as well. However, the reverse is not necessarily true; we cannot automatically grasp or comprehend *mom* merely through an understanding of *momjit*. In order to truly access *mom* one must first be "broken." This is a term I have discussed at length in my book *Buddhist Faith and Sudden Enlightenment*. The experience of being "broken" is one in which all the individual's conceptual and conditioned ways of perceiving himself and the universe have been discarded completely. This is the experience that occurs at the moment of enlightenment; it is what enables the individual to access a radically altered view of existence. Only through the experience of being "broken" can one adequately comprehend the invisible realm of *mom*. For those whose suffering is great, and for those who feel intensely the need to solve their own soteriological question, it is not difficult to become "broken." For them the problem is urgent, and they are thus willing to go to great lengths to find a solution, even if it means (which it does) abandoning all their previously held theories and opinions about themselves and the world.

Those who do not suffer are not really able to understand the religious suffering of others. When people become ill, however, or experience a personal tragedy of some sort, they will often look for an answer to their pain in the spiritual world, and it is there that they will begin to discover for the first time a sense of spiritual "health." In this sense, then, those who seem healthy, living ordinary lives, may be said to be spiritually "sick," as they have not yet accessed the deep inner world, the world of *mom*, which exists within them. A prolonged or terminal illness may thus remedy this situation, causing their inner eyes, which had previously been closed, to now open. Why is this? Perhaps it is because their selfishness has now disappeared. When one is healthy, he normally possesses a strong self-identity, often to the point of arrogance. If he becomes ill, however, this sense of self becomes weakened through his suffering, and once this protective shell is punctured, he becomes able to see the true picture of his life much more clearly.

In connection with this, I would like to tell you about a very well-educated man I know, who was sent to fight in the Korean War. He was assigned to a camp with many other soldiers who had had very little education—indeed, many of them could not even read or write. For three months my friend lived together with these men, eating and sharing the same sleeping quarters with them. During this time they all underwent an extensive military training. As my friend had nothing in common with the others outside of the sharing of their present circumstances, he had difficulty in establishing any real sense of communication with them. When the training was completed they were all sent into the battlefield. At one point they were attacked by North Korean soldiers, and although my friend and his comrades managed to escape, some of them were wounded in the skirmish. One of the men had broken his leg and my friend had to carry him on his back so that he could get safely back to camp. The journey was a lengthy one as the camp was quite a distance away, and they endured many hardships during their trek. Later, there was a second assault and this time my friend was injured in his shoulder. The very same comrade whom he had assisted earlier had recovered by this time, and so it was now his turn to carry my friend back to camp. This trek lasted for nine days; by the time they returned to camp, they both had to be hospitalized.

Each man, then, had saved the other's life. Since that time, their relationship was very unique; any difference that happened to arise between them was dismissed as being of no importance whatsoever. Prior to their shared experience on the battlefield, each had felt constantly irritated and annoyed by the behavior of the other. My friend had felt rather superior to the illiterate man and could not help seeing his actions as rather crude and ill-mannered, whereas the latter, in turn, felt extremely intimidated by my friend's intellectual achievements and elegant mannerisms. Yet following their ordeal they felt as if they were one body; each felt himself to be a part of the other.

Eventually, they were both discharged and sent home. Even after they ceased being military men, they still continued to maintain a correspondence. Twenty years passed, and yet there was no change in their relationship.

What is the meaning of this story? Through the sharing of each other's suffering, they were both able to penetrate and enter the realm of *mom*. Although they still continued to live rather ordinary lives in the mundane world of *momjit*, with all its distinctions and discriminations, this had very little, if any, effect on their relationship, for that part of their lives was deeply centered in *mom*.

Using another example to illustrate this same point, it is often the case that young married couples do a fair amount of bickering among themselves. They often come from different backgrounds, and may possess dissimilar sets of ideas, views, customs, and so forth. Yet as they continue to live together, sharing the experience of life itself with all its inherent conflict and pain (and joy as well), they will inevitably, inch by inch, gain closer access to the world of *mom*. In this way, their previous differences will seem to disappear as if into thin air, and as the years go by their relationship will deepen. The physical beauty of each partner may vanish, and the passion and excitement as well, but the relationship itself will improve as they begin to live within the realm of *mom*, where all such concerns are irrelevant.

We can see by these stories and examples that the *mom/momjit* paradigm may easily be applied to any aspect of human existence. One does not need to be a sage or practice meditation for many years in order to experience *mom*. Anyone and everyone can access its depths. In this sense, suffering may be seen as a blessing as it allows one an easy entrance into *mom's* world. The First Noble Truth of Buddhism is that life is suffering, yet the purpose of Buddhist practice is not to eliminate this suffering. As discussed earlier, when people are suffering they often turn to a spiritual or religious practice in an attempt to alleviate their pain. What happens, though, when one begins to immerse himself in a spiritual practice? He realizes not that his suffering can be eliminated but rather that he shares this experience with everyone else. He sees that all people suffer; it is the human condition. He later observes the suffering of an old person and a sick person, and he realizes that their pain is his as well. We all share this condition; it is not an isolated, occasional experience but rather an ongoing fact of life. To eliminate it is neither possible nor desirable, for it has a hidden value, which is that it can usher us into the realm of a vaster reality, that of *mom*. And *mom*, as we are beginning to learn, is a priceless treasure whose worth cannot be compared.

PRACTICAL APPLICATIONS

What can we do to alleviate our suffering? As I see it, there are three methods. One is through intellectual theory. This works only if the suffering is not too serious, and is usually applied in the consideration of others' pain. Another way is by adopting the attitude of a parent toward a child. This, of course, refers to suffering that is directly related to another person. Just as with intellectual theory, however, this method is not always effective. The third approach to suffering is the one I consider to be the best. Here, one applies the *mom/momjit* paradigm to his own life, by which he may understand that all phenomena are *momjit* and therefore impermanent. This awareness may help facilitate his return to the eternal source, *mom*. Upon this return back to *mom*, which is really a kind of reversal of his usual position, he may now realize that there is a unity between himself and the cause of his suffering, whether it be another person or a situation. The sense of separation from that which is causing him pain essentially disappears. Through his deepening awareness of this sense of unity, his suffering may gradually dissolve. As Jesus Christ said so simply in Matthew 19:19, "Love your neighbor as yourself."

We should note here that there is a difference between *mom* love and *momjit* love. With *momjit* love, you love someone for various external reasons. For example, they may fulfill your ideal of a good person, or they may do kind deeds for you. With *mom* love, however, you see the entire universe, and all the people in it, as yourself and you respond to its needs automatically, with gratitude and goodwill. It is like the right hand just naturally coming to the aid of the left. If one hand is in danger, the other one spontaneously jumps in to help, without any need for thought. This kind of love is very difficult to achieve, much less to maintain. Sometimes, when under great pressure or in an emergency, a person will respond in this way, such as when a mother jumps in front of an oncoming car in order to save her child from being struck by it.

When you return to *mom* you can no longer act from a *momjit* perspective because *mom* is now performing your actions for you. Actually, although we are not usually aware of it, *mom* is acting all the time, in every moment, always doing its best, without any expectation of reward. As it is the source from which all else arises, it enables all things to be accomplished. When the disciples asked Jesus how they could attain salvation, he replied, "With man this is impossible, but with God all things are possible" (Matthew 19:25–26). We may here substitute *momjit* for man and *mom* for God and say: with *momjit* it is not possible to achieve our goal; only with *mom* is it possible.

Society requires that we discipline ourselves in order to become successful. Yet our very use of such discipline can also place us in the deepest bondage, for the discipline has been externally generated and thus belongs to the realm of *momjit*. *Mom* can never be attained by using such methods; in order to reach it all our attachment to external remedies must be severed. Similarly, if a meditator is able to cut off his attachment to the *momjit* realm, he will undoubtedly gain access to the state of *samadhi*, that is, freedom from a dualistic way of thinking.

Most of us generally feel a great sense of separation between our minds and our bodies. We believe that the answers to our questions about life exist somewhere within our mental apparatus, and involve our belief systems and so forth.

This leads us to feel that our bodies have little, if any, relationship to our efforts to establish lasting peace in our lives. However, if we were to look a little deeper, we would discover that the truth of the matter is not quite so simple, for the fact is that our bodies actually have two aspects. On the one hand, they are as we see them, that is, vehicles through which we perform all of our daily activities, and lacking in any real sense of cohesiveness or purity. On the other hand, however, when we become aware, either through spiritual teachings or our own experience, of the fact of their essential impermanence, their lack of any real identity of their own, then we may begin to realize that they contain innumerable and immeasurable treasures within their depths, the likes of which we had never before imagined. The Hua-yen scriptures claim that the One is many. Viewed in this context, the body (the One) may be seen to contain the entire universe (the many) within it. It is truly wondrous; if we take the time and make the effort to listen to it, it will tell us all that we ever need to know. It can heal us by means of its omniscient awareness, but we must allow it to function as it will, without interference.

We may see from this that the teachings of Buddhism do not originate from some obscure, mystical, or abstract truth, but rather stem from what can be seen and experienced right in the present moment. By paying close attention to the messages of our bodies, we can be in constant contact with the truth of any situation or experience. The truth is always close at hand; indeed, it is immanent. The fact that it may be uncovered in this way shows us that our bodies represent not only the ordinary, visible aspect of *mom*, but its religious or hidden aspect as well. The truth of any matter is nothing other than this invisible aspect of *mom*, which, as we said, may be accessed by means of the body.

STAGES OF ACCESS

Gaining such access to *mom* is not an easy matter, however; several steps are required. For our purposes here, we may describe three stages or levels (Sanskrit: *bhumis*) which must be passed through or attained, sequentially, in order to experience the hidden aspect of *mom*. At the outset, it must be recognized that we need to relinquish our attachment to *momjit*, to all of our bodily functions; this includes the five senses as well as the mind. In this context, the mind is considered part of the mind/body complex, as opposed to the invisible realm of *mom*, which transcends mind and body. We need to understand that it is not our minds or our bodies that cause us difficulties, but rather our attachment to them, that is to say, our tendency to view them as fixed entities, which we can control in any way we like. This is a grave misunderstanding on our part and therefore it is in Stage One that we need to learn how to diminish the role which our minds and bodies play in our life. Yet a preliminary step is necessary here if we are to find the strength and depth of vision needed to break our deep-seated attachments. This first step is the cultivation of a firm foundation of understanding concerning the nature and existence of *mom* itself. It is crucial that one be cognizant of the fact that there is an alternative to his suffering. This is why all religions place such a strong emphasis on the invisible world, proclaiming its wondrous glory. Without some glimmer of awareness of this world, which Western religions term God and Eastern thought labels emptiness, how can we ever hope to loosen our desperate grip on the mundane, material realm? Therefore, in Stage One the fact that there indeed does exist an invisible yet universal aspect of reality, which we are calling *mom*, is strongly emphasized. At the same time, our awareness of *momjit*, the world of our bodies and minds as well as the myriad objects within our perception, must be either substantially minimized or else completely negated. Again, the strategy here is that by stressing the universal, *mom*, one's attachment to his own individual suffering may be reduced. As we can see, at this stage the differences between *mom* and *momjit*, the universal and the individual, are asserted clearly. In Buddhist terms, in order to be able to detach ourselves from the *sahā* world of suffering, we need to be made aware of the existence of the *sukha* world of bliss. According to one sect of Buddhism, this *sukha* world actually exists as the Pure Land to which practitioners will return following their death on the earthly plane. Western religions similarly espouse the greatness and invincibility of God (*mom*) as compared with the weakness and sinfulness of man (*momjit*), and offer us the Kingdom of Heaven if we atone for our wrongdoings.

Stage Two begins when we have more or less attained a certain level of detachment from *momjit*. This achievement enables us to discover for ourselves the existence of *mom* in its hidden aspect, which had previously eluded us. For practitioners of Western religions, to detach from self-concerns is to enter into the presence of God. For Buddhists, elimination of attachment represents an embarkment onto the path of enlightenment and indeed may lead directly to an experience of awakening, in however small or large a degree. Yet the danger of this stage is that just as we were previously attached to *momjit* and material concerns, now we may similarly become identified with our new-found awareness of *mom*, whether it be of God or of emptiness. This kind of attachment, if we persist in it, can create many problems in our daily lives. It is vital that we realize that this is not the final, ultimate understanding. Hopefully, we will be able to discern this error when it occurs so that we may summon the courage and determination to continue and complete our journey.

Stage Three, the final stage, is reached when we find within ourselves the means to throw off all attachment to *mom*. As implied above, this may not be an easy task, but it is a necessary one. It is this ability to negate both *momjit* and *mom* (defined as double negation in Buddhist thought) that enables us to see these two aspects in their correct relationship to each other. This relationship is one of nonduality, in which each exists within the other. At this stage, then, the Buddhist lives not as one who has merely had an enlightenment experience, but rather as the embodiment of enlightenment itself. He is not just a human being, but a living example of truth. The follower of Western religion will no longer consider himself to be a devotee of God; instead, he will have so completely merged with God that he lives not his own life but God's will. Thus, it becomes evident that at this stage all *momjit*, and this includes ourselves, exists as a manifestation or expression of the deeper, hidden *mom*. The *momjit* that is now perceived will differ markedly from the *momjit* of the previous stages: one who has attained this stage can for the first time see *momjit* in its entirety, for *mom* is now realized as being included within it. Thus, as we discussed in the beginning of this section, the body is not merely a framework for our flesh and bones, but contains within it an entire universe of possibilities and existences. People who have reached this level of understanding live ordinary lives in the everyday world, and on the surface may appear no different from anyone else. Yet whatever they say or do will be a direct reflection of *mom*, universality, rather than of *momjit*, or mere self-concern.

In terms of the Christian religion, our reading of the Bible shows us that Jesus lived at the level of Stage Three. He was keenly aware of his oneness with God, his Father. At various times in his life he proclaimed, "I am in the Father, and the Father is in me" (John 14:10). At the end of his life, when he was arrested by the Pharisees, he told them to read the scriptures, which stated that anyone who had a message from God was considered a Son of God. In essence, he was saying that everyone possesses the seed of oneness with God within himself. This is a clear recognition of nonduality on the part of Jesus. Furthermore, we may note the statement in Genesis that all humans are created in the image of God, yet another indication of the Judeo-Christian awareness of nonduality (Genesis 1:27).

In Buddhism, of course, the invisible aspect of *mom* is not perceived in such a personal way, that is, as a Creator or a Father, but rather is seen to exist on a more abstract level, as depicted by the use of such terms as emptiness, *nirvāṇa*, suchness, and so forth. This is due to the vast differences in both the culture and language of the people of East Asia as compared to the inhabitants of areas farther to the West. However, although East Asians were quite liberated in their understanding of nonduality, this did not, and does not now, necessarily help them to reach their soteriological goal, which is access to the realm of *mom*. They often remain helplessly trapped within the intellectual dimension of understanding, failing to realize nonduality on an experiential level. For those who struggle with this difficulty, the cultivation of faith may prove to be of invaluable assistance, for one who has faith possesses a deep inner sense of clarity, conviction, and certainty about his world that far surpasses a merely intellectual, rational understanding. One possessing faith carries within him an awareness of "existential nonduality," which is essentially an experiential embodiment of truth. One whose understanding is limited to "conceptual nonduality" will by contrast be sorely lacking in the necessary experiential dimension of awareness that is necessary if he wishes to access *mom*.

THE COEXISTENCE OF *MOM* AND *MOMJIT*

Earlier we spoke of *mom* as having two aspects, the absolute or religious and the visible, ordinary aspect. We may also use the terms *universal* and *individual* to identify these two facets of *mom*. In each case, the former aspect refers to the indefinable realm or, in Christian terms, the realm of God. What, then, is the ordinary or individual *mom*? One way of looking at it is to call it the enlightened person's testimony. In the Gospel of St. John, Jesus claims, "I am in the Father, and the Father is in me" (John 14:10). Here, the Father, or God, may be seen as the universal *mom*, whereas "me" refers to the individual *mom*. This individual *mom* is actually no other than *momjit*, or everything we can experience with our six senses.

The question that most often arises at this point is this: How can it be that universal *mom* and individual *mom* are considered to coexist simultaneously, as Jesus asserted in the above quote? A similar question would be: How can my body, which is said to represent *mom*, be taken as the universal or transcendental aspect of reality? We may approach this issue from two different vantage points. The first is a thought process and begins with the assumption that there does indeed exist a universal body or reality, which Christians call God. This assumption will naturally require a certain level of faith on the part of the individual. In the Hua-yen Sūtra of Buddhism, the metaphor of Indra's net is used to help people understand this more deeply. Indra's net is said to be composed of many pearls; the significance of this net is that each individual pearl is seen to be reflected in all other pearls, and at the same time all of the other pearls are reflected within one single pearl. In this sense, then, we may say that one is in the many, and the many are in one. A simpler version of this idea would be, "One is all, and All is One." Translated into personal terms, when all others are included in me, my own boundaries disappear. I have been so expanded that I am infinity itself. Therefore, "I" do not exist as separate and apart from the others, for it is they that contribute to my existence, my identity. If their reflection did not exist within me, I would not be "me." This, of course, is a Buddhist concept. Jesus himself did not venture this far.

This is one of the key differences between Buddhism and Christianity: whereas Buddhism, and East Asian Buddhism in particular, directly asserts the mutual identity of the one and the many, Christianity merely alludes to such a fact, but does not state it as a truth. It is tempting to speculate as to the reasons for such a disparity between the two religions. One contributing factor may be the difference in lifestyle between the followers of each religion. The culture of the Middle Eastern area where Jesus was born and lived was a nomadic one. The lives of the people living there were full of insecurity, as they were constantly on the move, pulling up stakes in one place and settling down in a new, completely unfamiliar territory. Those living in such a way would naturally feel the need for a supportive, all-encompassing Protector who would keep them from danger by providing a sense of stability and safety. The culture of East Asia, on the other hand, was by and large an agricultural one. The majority of those people were farmers who spent their whole lives in one location, diligently tilling their fields in order to supply food for their family and community. Such people had much less of a need for divine protection, at least in a geographical sense, and were freer to let their thoughts wander toward more abstract types of philosophical speculation.

To return to our discussion, we have said that one way to understand the close relationship between individual and universal *mom* is through a recognition of the basic sense of oneness that pervades throughout the universe. If I am in the Father, then I must somehow partake of whatever my Father partakes; we both participate in the same reality. Similarly, if one pearl is reflected in all the others, then that pearl naturally has an existence that is intimately connected to the others.

The second way of approaching this issue is to begin not with a philosophical premise but with reality itself, that is, the human condition in contemporary society. The first thing we must keep in mind here is that we live in a competitive world. We are constantly being evaluated by others and pressured to conform to their expectations from the very moment of our birth. Our parents watch our every move to make sure that it is in strict accordance with their standards, and when we become old enough to go to school, we are similarly assessed by our teachers and prospective friends. This occurs again and again throughout our lives: when we attend college, look for a job, get married, and so forth. This pressure to conform must give rise to at least a certain amount of deception on our part at some time or another. We are taught not to show our real emotions, but rather to always smile and look happy. The conflict we will inevitably feel between our inner and outer worlds can generate much tension in our lives; this we have all experienced.

TWO DIMENSIONS OF HUMAN EXISTENCE

We each have two dimensions: our intelligence, with which we are aware and which manifests as our visible karma, and our physical body, which is neutral and has no concern with how intelligent we are, or how rich or poor. These two dimensions are often in conflict with each other, causing us great suffering. The first is a reflection of *momjit*, as it concerns the external functions of our body, that is, the use of our various senses, including the mind, in order to achieve our goals. The second dimension, the body itself, is *mom*. When we compromise our internal world in order to conform to the needs and desires of the external society, who is the victim? It is *mom*, our body, which is the victim, which suffers. Universal *mom* is unchanging, eternal, but individual *mom*, our body, can eventually be destroyed if it is subjected to this kind of conflict unceasingly, over a long period of time.

We may say that greed (which is one particularized manifestation of *momjit*) is ruled by utilitarian concerns. *Mom*, the truth or higher understanding, is not involved here; only one's personal benefit is considered. *Mom* has its own order, its own laws, in which benefit, or utilitarianism, plays no part. This order may be called by various names, such as life, truth, nature, and so forth. In ancient Rome it was called "the way." Roads were very important even in ancient times, for they were the only "way" by which people could get from one place to another. We have all heard the phrase, "All roads lead to Rome." Jesus said, in the Gospel of St. John, "I am the way and the truth and the life" (John 14:6). These three characteristics of *mom* represent the *mom* that epitomized each of the three cultures of Jesus' time: the "way" represented the highest value for the Romans, the "truth" was a vital concern in Greek culture, and "life" was given the highest priority by the Hebrews. In St. John's mind, then, Jesus embraced the deepest, most esteemed virtues of each culture. My personal preference is for the word *life*; I see it as embracing both external nature and my individual physical body. I think it is self-evident that utilitarianism is not life's concern; life's concern is universality, the totality of inner and outer existence.

To reiterate: there is a conflict between our two dimensions: our intelligence and our body. They do not harmonize easily. If they were able to do so, we would then be in a state of enlightenment, *mom*. As we discussed earlier, when you are able to return to *mom*, then all *momjit* simultaneously becomes the *momjit* of *mom*. Thus, if we wish to return to *mom*, we must first be aware of the problems caused by *momjit*, our intelligence. If the utilitarian self is seen as primary, there will be no way for us to discover (or uncover) *mom*. What is required on our part at this point of understanding is a kind of inner revolution, in which all false *momjit* based on utilitarianism is attacked. This may be labeled the first revolution, which was earlier identified as Stage One. Buddhism often makes use of various negative expressions, such as *neti, neti* (not this, not that), the neither-nor paradigm, Nāgārjuna's famous eight negations,[1] and so forth. These systems all pertain to one's state of mind at the first revolution. They represent the means used to negate all language as well as all concepts in order to aid the individual in destroying the false *momjit*. This does not mean to imply that language has no value; it is rather that this initial step is necessary in order for us to reach a position in which language (and concepts) is not creating a false reality, a false truth. Once our revolution has been successfully carried out, then we may revert back to language, at which time our perspective will have changed completely and our use of language will have changed as well.

At the second revolution, or Stage Two, Buddha is born within you. This means that you have successfully returned to *mom*. Now all language, and all manifestations of *momjit*, are accepted as useful and indeed valuable. Both success and failure are welcomed; each is seen as a reflection of the Buddha's innate wisdom.

We can see that the scenes at Stage One and Stage Two are entirely different. In Stage One, the first revolution, only negative terms are employed. All other language is considered not only irrelevant, but also misleading. We follow the Middle Way: we go neither left nor right, we practice neither capitalism nor communism, and so forth. At the second revolution, however, all language is accepted; we may go either left or right. In fact, we may go both left and right, as each reflects the truth in its own way. This may be said to be accomplished by the light of Buddha's wisdom.

CHAPTER TWO

Tools for Transformation

THE NEED FOR TRANSFORMATION

It is very important for us to realize that whatever perception of *mom* we have, it will by its very nature be limited. Our understanding of the transcendent realm of *mom* is a creative construction erected entirely by our minds and does not represent its true reality. Only at enlightenment can this creating habit of ours be stopped, for at that moment we will ourselves become the universal self, *mom*. In actuality, this universal self is nothing other than the individual self; when we become transformed at the moment of enlightenment, we can experience this.

How can someone who does not believe in the experience of transformation become a believer? He will need to have a "death" experience of some sort. Our physical death, the death of the body, is viewed in East Asian Buddhist thought as a "small death." Before the body dies, however, we are given many opportunities to experience the "great death," which is transformation or enlightenment itself.

Many people, including religious practitioners, do not view death objectively. Christians often believe that someone is waiting at the gates of heaven to usher them in. Similarly, Pure Land Buddhists envision themselves entering a blissful realm, filled with beautiful lights and colors. I believe, however that it is imperative that we search for a deeper understanding of the significance of death. If we fail to face this matter now, while we are still alive, then we are failing to confront our life as it exists in this very moment, for every moment of each life contains within it this added dimension. This is what we do not wish to face, for it is here that we have formed our deepest attachment to *momjit*.

THE USE OF THE *HWADU*

One very powerful way of looking into the matter of our death is through the use of a *hwadu*. The practice of working with a *hwadu* has traditionally been undertaken by the Zen Buddhists in East Asian countries, and most notably in China, Japan, and Korea. This word, which is more popularly known as the Japanese term *kōan*, refers to a seemingly nonsensical question or phrase prescribed by a Zen master to his students. The student is asked to meditate with this phrase, absorbing its flavor as much as he is able, in the hopes of arriving at a suitable response, which he then presents to his master for approval. There are approximately 1,700 *hwadu* in existence; some popular examples are: "What is your original face before you were born?" "What is the sound of one hand clapping?" "Who am I?" and "What is this?" The purpose of *hwadu* practice is for the practitioner to break through his ordinary, conceptual mode of perception and understanding, so that he may experience in a flash of insight (or enlightenment) reality as it is in its totality: indescribable, unidentifiable, inexpressible, and untainted by thought. This, of course, is the realm of *mom*, and entry into its domain is no easy matter. What is required of the practitioner is no less than the "death" of his mind, with all its cherished concepts about life and existence. In the process he will inevitably encounter many doubts as well as innumerable other obstacles. The procedure may be compared to learning how to ride a bicycle: one will fall down many, many times but eventually, if he persists in his efforts, he will learn not only how to stay on but to experience all the benefits that follow. To offset his doubts, however, it is vital that the practitioner have faith in his teacher. He must have total respect for him. For many, this represents an obstacle in itself: How many people are willing or able to maintain that kind of trust? Thus, an internal need, a sort of existential demand, on the part of the practitioner is very important. If his need is strong enough, he will have an easier time with trusting. As a saying goes: if you are sick, you will seek the medicine.

With regard to the matter of doubt, mentioned above, we may say that there are two kinds of doubts. The first includes certain anxieties about one's teacher or one's spiritual path as well as insecurities about one's own ability to succeed in his spiritual endeavors. Although these kinds of doubts have no relevance to one's spiritual quest, they can cause the practitioner many difficulties within the course of his *hwadu* practice. The second kind of doubt, however, is not only useful but necessary. Here, the word *doubt* refers more closely to the terms *question* or *investigate*. It implies a willingness to involve oneself 100 percent in the task of working with his *hwadu*, allowing it to live alongside of him both day and night, so that he himself becomes the *hwadu*. If this practice is carried out correctly, he will gradually loosen his grasp on worldly matters to the point that he eventually "dies" to all his usual thought processes. He will begin to live in such a way that he becomes completely engulfed by the words of the *hwadu* themselves. In relation to this, Wŏnhyo has stated: "[E]xternally they forget all truths and internally they search for their own minds. This is why they are able to reach the truthless ultimate truth."[1]

However, as discussed above, it is important that the practitioner balance this deep questioning with an equally profound faith. If one merely doubts without believing in the possibility of a breakthrough to enlightenment, he will remain a skeptic. If, on the other hand, he is a believer who has no doubts, he is in danger of becoming a fundamentalist, an extremist. What is the kind of faith needed here? Basically, it is the ability or willingness to believe that the teacher may be trusted and that the long lineage of Zen masters has a personal significance for him. In this sense, then, *hwadu* meditation can be viewed as the arena for the conflict between faith in what the teacher says (i.e., that you are a Buddha) and doubts about yourself (i.e., that you are not a Buddha). The practitioner must wrestle with these two seemingly opposing forces continuously, as first one, then the other, holds sway. Eventually, when the time is appropriate, he will find that they become reconciled. This, however, requires great determination and perseverance, propelled by one's deep inner need, as described earlier.

The paradox of *hwadu* practice is that one must not seek the literal meaning of the *hwadu*. In fact, just the opposite effort is required: the practitioner must abandon all his usual modes of thought and perception in order to apprehend the intended message of the *hwadu's* riddle. With regard to this, the noted Korean monk Chinul (1158–1210) has discussed the advantage of using what he calls the "live word" during *hwadu* practice, as opposed to the "dead word." By "live word" he means the bare words of the *hwadu* itself, whereas "dead word" refers to all the thoughts or concepts one might entertain with regard to the words of the *hwadu*. Chinul asserts that the realm of enlightenment, *mom*, cannot be accessed through the use of the "dead word"; rather, *mom's* mysterious essence can only be penetrated when approached through the "live word." It is only through deep, consistent questioning of the words themselves, rather than the conjuring up of thoughts about the words or their meaning, that one may sufficiently detach himself from *momjit*. Thus, if one is working with the *hwadu* "What is my original face before I was born?" he should not think about what he was like before his birth, or visualize various faces or images of a possible previous existence. Rather, he needs to focus 100 percent of his attention and energy on the words of the question itself, and allow these words to enter him deeply. Chinul says:

> From the beginning, followers of the shortcut Son [Japanese: Zen] approach who have gained entrance remain unaffected by acquired understanding in regard to both dharma and its attributes. Straight off, they take up a task-less *hwadu* and are concerned only with raising it to their attention and focusing on it. For this reason, they remain free of ratiocination via mind or consciousness or the way of speech or the way of meaning and stay clear of any idea of a time sequence in which views, learning, understanding, or conduct are to be developed.[2]

If the practitioner permits the words of his *hwadu* to absorb him completely, he will eventually reach a state in which he feels he can move neither forward nor backward. He experiences this as a kind of "death" state; yet if he continues in his efforts, at some point he will suddenly find himself breaking through this impasse in a shattering moment of awareness or insight. In this way, he will have attained the realm of *mom*, the enlightenment state.

INITIAL THOUGHTS ON *HWADU* PRACTICE: THE THREE DISCIPLINES

At this time, I would like to elaborate on the matter of *hwadu* practice, as such a practice, if applied with an attitude of both firm conviction and perseverance, can lead one to directly experience the invisible realm of *mom*. More and more people are becoming familiar with the term "*hwadu* meditation," yet what many people may not be aware of is that this type of spiritual practice, if performed correctly, actually involves three basic disciplines: (1) harmonization of the body, (2) harmonization of the breath, and (3) harmonization of the mind. Let's look at each one individually. The first, harmonization of the body, can itself be further divided into three aspects. The most fundamental requirement, which acts as a basis for the other two, is the adoption of a correct sitting position. If the practitioner is relatively flexible, he can assume the traditional lotus or half-lotus position. If he has stiff joints or other concerns that make those positions difficult, he may sit on a chair with his feet flat on the floor. The most important thing is that his spine be erect, which is the second aspect of body harmonization. Without an erect spine, it will be more difficult for the air to flow freely throughout one's body as he breathes in and out. The third aspect, that of relaxation, is extremely important, and is often neglected or overlooked, even by experienced meditators. We all carry around a lot of tension in our bodies due to the stresses of modern-day life; this tension must be released as much as possible. It usually centers around the area of the head, neck, and shoulders; however, some meditation techniques involve a process of successively isolating and relaxing each and every section of the body, from head to toe.

The second discipline of *hwadu* meditation, harmonization of the breath, is often referred to as *t'an-t'ien* breathing. The term *t'an-t'ien* may be translated as "red field," and refers to the area in the body located one and a half inches below the navel. This area acts as a storehouse for all of our energy: the energy naturally collects here and is then distributed throughout the rest of the body. The harmonization of one's inhalations and exhalations as performed in *t'an-t'ien* breathing is of vital concern to the practitioner of *hwadu* meditation. Our breathing must be conducted properly if we are to correctly reflect the universal order. In these stressful, fast-paced modern times, we are all constantly acting in ways that oppose this natural, smooth-flowing order of the universe. In order to meet the demands of our competitive world, we often end up, whether consciously or not, fostering a certain amount of greed. If this greed is not satisfied, then anger and other emotions begin to arise. This negativity can be rectified through proper breathing. If we observe an infant sleeping, we will notice that its exhalations are slightly longer than its inhalations. Elderly people as well, upon the completion of their worldly duties and as they enter their final years, usually manifest this kind of breathing. As meditators, it is in our best interests to cultivate such a practice. The instructions for *t'an-t'ien* breathing, then, are as follows: inhale through your nose, sending the breath down into the *t'an-t'ien*, and hold it there for a few seconds. Then release it, allowing it to come back up and out again through the nose. It is important to breathe softly, so that a feather held up to the nose would not move. As each breath is completed, we assign it a number, beginning with "one," and with each successive outbreath we mentally say the next number, until we reach "ten." Then we begin the process all over again, counting each breath from one to ten. If you can maintain your count from one to ten without getting sidetracked by wandering thoughts, then you are indeed well trained. If thoughts arise, you will forget your breathing practice, and will need to start the process all over again.

According to herbal medicine as practiced in East Asia, the body has two energies: a cool, water energy and a warm, fire energy. These two energies must be well harmonized and properly distributed to every part of the body. In our modern society these energies are usually out of balance, due to the three poisons of greed, anger, and ignorance. The fire energy tends to rise into the head, making one easily angered and disturbed, and often causing headaches. The antidote to such an imbalance is to learn how to send the fire energy downward, replacing it with the cooler water energy. This may be accomplished through *t'an-t'ien* meditation. Sending cool, moist water energy up toward the head helps one to think more clearly and calmly. Conversely, bringing the warm, dry fire energy down into the lower body helps alleviate sexual desire and combats illnesses that originate in this region.

The third aspect of *hwadu* meditation, harmonization of the mind, is the culminating step of this three-part process. When we hear the term "harmonizing the mind," we may think this refers to various ethical, moral, philosophical, or religious teachings. However, the most important concern of *hwadu* meditation is to learn how to free one's mind from all attachments. When we do this, we are practicing what is called *"wu-nien"* in Chinese, which translates as "no-thought." This term is not easy for one to understand, especially for people not familiar with Chinese characters and their symbolism. What do we mean by "no-thought?"

The Zen school often refers to the Platform Sūtra when discussing this term. This sūtra, although not written by the Buddha, affirms the Buddhist ideal of transcending one's intellect so that one may attain the state of "no-thought." It is customary for a Zen master to give his student a *hwadu* to help him in his practice; as discussed earlier, with the use of this tool, he may more easily release his conditionings and mental attachments. The word *hwadu* translates as "public issue"; however, the issue to be considered is neither governmental nor social, but rather relates to the religious world. In this world, the most important issue is that of birth and death. Everyone is concerned with this matter, as it affects all of us. No one knows when or how death will come, but we all know that it comes to everyone. The *hwadu* deals directly with this unavoidable truth, yet it does not do so by the means of the intellect. *Hwadu* meditation lies beyond the realm of the intellect altogether; it points directly to the world of *mom*.

One of the most popular *hwadu* is the *hwadu mu*. It goes like this: A student approached Zen master Chao-chou and asked, "Does

a dog have the Buddha-nature?" (Buddha-nature is an eternally existing inherent state that enables one to attain enlightenment.) Master
Chao-chou said, "*Mu!*" which translates as "No" or "Not." Why did
Chao-chou say this? The practitioner who is assigned this *hwadu* by
his master must ask himself this question unceasingly during his
meditation, yet he must not use his intellect in doing so. If he is
persistent, then eventually his consciousness will separate itself from
worldly concerns. He will become pacified, attaining a state in which
no thoughts will have access. Then, according to causes and conditions, he may attain enlightenment.

NO-THOUGHT

Let's look a little more closely at this term *wu-nein*, or "no-thought."
What does this term really mean? The state of no-thought is extolled
by Buddhist practitioners as representing the epitome of attainment.
Yet how can one carry on his daily activities in such a state? Is
it possible?

We must first of all understand that the word *no* in this context
should not be taken to mean the opposite of *yes*. Rather, the word
no is used to eliminate the tumor of our dualistic way of thinking.
"No" reflects the emptiness that lies directly underneath or beyond
our thought. When thoughts are severed by this "no," then true reality, also called *tathatā* (translated as "suchness") appears. Theistically
speaking, this reality may be called God. God is the essence, the true
reality, or *mom* from which all thinking is produced. The thinking
itself is *momjit*, as discussed earlier. Looking at the term *wu-nien*, *wu*
may be equated with *mom* or "essence" or "true reality," whereas *nien*
is *momjit* or "manifestation," and refers to not only our thoughts but
also our speech, actions, and indeed all phenomena. *Mom* as reflected
in the term *wu* acts in a negative manner, enabling us to eliminate
our incorrect, thought-based way of existing.

Before the Tun-huang version of the Platform Sūtra was discovered in the 1930s, the only known record of this sūtra was the
Koshoji version. In this latter version, the translator has interpreted
the Chinese characters to read, "Thought means thinking of what?"
This translation represents a dualistic, and thus incorrect, understanding. In saying "thought means thinking . . . ," the word "thinking" is
used as a transitive verb and thus requires an object. In other words,
we need to say, "thinking of what?" Any construction that involves a
subject and/or object is inherently dualistic and thus does not conform
to true reality, suchness, or *mom*.

What, then, is *nien* or "thought"? In a theistic context, we may say that thought is a function of God. It is what is produced by true reality itself. This is a very straightforward interpretation of the term *nien* and leaves no doubt in our mind as to its meaning. This is the meaning that is conveyed in the Tun-huang version; this version correctly omits the word *thinking* altogether. Rather, it merely asks, "What is thought?" The answer it then gives is, "Thoughts are the function of True Reality." In the Koshoji version, after asking the question, "Thought means thinking of what?" it goes on to proclaim, "Thought means thinking of the original nature of true reality." This, again, is a dualistic statement, as it again includes the verb "thinking," which as a transitive verb requires an object. In this Koshoji version, then, the tumor of dualism is not eliminated. Rather, the translator has the practitioner still seeking after suchness; the enlightened Buddha is still looking for Buddha. In Zen, it is understood that as soon as the clouds are gone, the sun is automatically seen to be shining. It is not that the clouds first go away, and then the sun shines. Rather, the two events occur simultaneously. In the Koshoji version, the practitioner is still searching for the sun after the clouds have gone away. Thus, the *mom* message of inclusiveness and nonduality has been changed to a *momjit* message of separation and opposition. The vital *mom* understanding which reflects the natural order of things is absent, leaving us with a distorted view of reality. In the Tun-huang version, however, all duality has been eliminated and *momjit*, or one's thoughts, is correctly seen as an inherently operating function of true reality. This is the crucial message of *mom*: thoughts do not oppose reality but are rather a natural occurrence operating in tandem with it.

Scholars as well as practitioners need to be careful when reading this text, and understand that once the *mom* message of nonduality is clarified, then the *momjit* message concerning the nature of our thoughts is naturally included. There can be no separation of the two in our minds, as they intrinsically do not exist apart from one another. This is the essential theme underlying all Buddhist teachings; we must be clear in our own understanding of this vital message and realize its significance for our lives.

GETTING DOWN TO PRACTICE

Faith and Doubt

Regarding one's practice, whatever spiritual or religious practice or preparation one has undertaken prior to using the *hwadu* is useless and irrelevant. In theistic language, it may similarly be said that nothing can adequately prepare you for your meeting with God, for in front of God all preconceived ideas and understandings are of no account. This is not to say that they should be criticized or looked at as wrong—it is just that they do not apply; they are of no avail.

At the moment that you begin your questioning with the *hwadu*, at the moment you begin to ask, for example, "Why did Chao-chou say *mu*?" nothing else should be in your mind, either positive, negative, or neutral. This is the nature of doubt; it is not mystic or tantric or esoteric. At the moment you begin questioning, you are perfectly enlightened; you are Buddha. However, at this time you will undoubtedly encounter various distractions emanating from your mind. This is why most people need the support of a group, or at least a regular daily practice, as well as certain rules, regulations, and so forth.

The investigation of four dimensions is necessary for the spiritual development of any individual. The first is the moral dimension. This is fundamental; without a strong code of ethics one will not be able to make any progress on the spiritual path. The second dimension is that of philosophy. All of us, whether we are illiterate merchants or accomplished professionals, seek an essential truth or understanding about life which we may rely upon. The third dimension is the area of religion, which embodies such issues as "Where did I come from?" and "Where am I going?" This dimension is concerned with beginnings and endings, or birth and death, and is reflected by the various creation stories and eschatological theories. Finally, there is the formless dimension as investigated through the study and practice of Zen. This dimension can never be adequately understood through words or our mental faculties; it can only be approached through such practices as *hwadu* meditation.

The word *doubt* is represented by the letter "*i*" in Chinese and is pronounced "ee." Its meaning cannot be easily grasped by beginners, for its connotation is not a negative one, as it is in Western translations. When one questions with the *hwadu*, this "*i*" turns into *tuan*, which originally meant "group," but now has come to mean "accumulation," as in a snowball that grows larger and larger as it continues to roll through the snow. *Tuan*, then, refers to a group or accumulation of "*i*," or doubt. When a practitioner first starts working with the *hwadu*, his "*i*" is very fragile; it has no real power and is easily interrupted or broken. However, as the meditator continues with his practice, the opposite effect occurs; the doubt becomes stronger and stronger, growing in intensity with each practice. Eventually, this doubt sensation will not disappear even after the meditator has ended his period of formal practice. The practitioner will then find that his doubt cannot be eliminated from any aspect of his daily life; thus, while he is eating, or taking a shower, or talking with his colleagues, the doubt is right there with him. It continues to grow, becoming as large as the earth itself. As time passes, it becomes even larger, expanding to encompass the entire universe. Eventually, everything becomes enveloped by this ball of doubt. It is at this stage that one may be said to possess total concentration.

We all have various pragmatic or utilitarian concerns; this is a natural part of being human. Yet when we doubt or question with the *hwadu*, we are free from this utilitarian attitude. We need not attempt to eliminate our utilitarian concepts or actions in an effort to purify ourselves—all we need to do is doubt. Since this doubt or "*i*" is larger than the universe itself, it can best be understood as reflecting the realm of *mom*, the invisible, formless world. At the moment that you begin to raise the doubt, your *mom* is working. Actually, it is always working, regardless of our efforts or beliefs, but when we begin to question with the *hwadu*, the *mom* realm becomes more accessible to our consciousness.

For one who begins to work with the *hwadu*, three qualities are of vital importance: (1) faith in the teachings of the Buddha and Zen masters, (2) determination, or our confidence in the potential power of the *hwadu* itself, and (3) doubt, which here performs the meritorious and virtuous function of freeing us from all our negative, ingrained habits, such as pride, greed, anger, and so forth. Our worst enemy in this context is our expectation, or our hope for certain results, which again stems from our age-old conceptualizations and intellectualizations. In the meantime, however, there is no harm in making use of various other techniques, such as yoga, tai chi, breath control, chanting, and so forth. Such techniques may help us remedy certain imbalances in our bodies and/or minds. We need to be clear in our understanding, however, that *hwadu* meditation lies beyond the realm of time and thus is also beyond causality. It is not meant to serve as a remedy for anything; its practice is not meant to bring us any gain or benefit. "What is the purpose then?" you may ask. It has none; it merely functions as a pointer to the formless, invisible realm of *mom*.

Faith and Surrender

When a Christian encounters God, he or she considers it to be an event of monumental significance. The East Asian Buddhist practice of raising doubt through the *hwadu* can and should be viewed in a similar way. In order to understand what this means, let us consider the world of Chao-chou, the Zen master who answered *"Mu"* to his disciple's question, "Does a dog have the Buddha-nature?"

We need first of all to understand that Chao-chou's world was predominantly Buddhist. During the Tang dynasty in China, in which Chao-chou lived, the most powerful and respected institution was the Buddhist monastery. All of the intellectual elite gathered together by way of the world of Buddhist thought and practice. Chao-chou himself was trusted implicitly as a representative of great wisdom. This atmosphere of awe and reverence is entirely different from the feeling that modern people have for their leaders in today's world, whether religious or secular. We have been trained intellectually, and thus we constantly compare one leader, or one political or religious system, to another. In the process of making such comparisons, which really reflects a kind of questioning or doubt, we are making use of our six sense organs. Each organ involved is employed to help bring us closer to a decision or judgment. Thus, the eye will enable us to see something more clearly, the ear will help us to hear better, and so forth.

In the case of *hwadu* meditation, however, the six sense organs are essentially given a death sentence; they are not permitted to function in any way whatsoever. Thus, all of one's faculties are rendered useless at the time of raising doubt with the *hwadu*. No matter what you have seen, heard, smelled, tasted, touched, or thought—it is all of no avail to you now. This does not mean that you become blind, deaf, or dumb, however. Actually, once you truly surrender your normal use of these faculties, they become able to perceive things which were previously unknown to them.

How is the practitioner able to surrender all his sense faculties? It is at this point that most people become apprehensive—no one wants to undergo such a "death." It must be remembered, however, that death also means resurrection, and once we let go of one thing, another will arise in its place. There is a Zen story that is often told in relation to this issue of surrender. A seeker is told by his teacher that his journey requires him to travel eastward, and that he must continually move in that direction. So the seeker dutifully starts out, walking down a well-paved, well-traveled road. Eventually, however, the road narrows to become just a dirt path, and then the path itself disappears. The seeker begins to encounter various disagreeable and unsettling events and phenomena, such as snakes, tigers, floods, poison ivy, and so forth. He has been told to keep going, however, so he continues on. At last he comes to a dead end: he has arrived at a sharp cliff that overlooks a deep abyss. At the top of the cliff, reaching down over the abyss is a tree that is broken apart and dangling over the edge. The seeker knows that he must somehow reach the bottom of the cliff, and the only way to do so is to grasp onto the tree, which may help carry him down. Yet when he grasps onto the tree, he realizes that it will only take him part of the way down, and that to reach the bottom, he must let go of the tree. However, if he lets go of the tree, he will fall into the abyss below. What should he do?

Symbolically, we can see that there is no salvation for him if he continues to hold onto the tree—there is no means of rescue provided by such an act. Yet if he lets go of the tree, death seems certain: the distance between the tree and the bottom of the cliff is too great to ensure survival. If he can let go of his grasp, however, his own death will lead to a resurrection. This is what is promised both by the Zen masters and by all those who have chosen faith as their spiritual foundation. It is only faith that enables us to surrender in such a situation. Those who lack faith, however, either continue holding onto the tree or else they retreat, retracing their steps and returning back to their old, familiar territory.

A similar dilemma will arise when one practices with the *hwadu*. When raising a question such as "Why did Chao-chou say '*Mu*'?" you are entirely cut off from past and future. As your time system is completely broken, you find you have nothing upon which you can rely. To say or affirm "I am Buddha" at this point is worthless; actually, it is worse than worthless, for it means that you have strayed from your absorption in your question and have instead reentered the world of mere intellectualization. What do you do at this moment? How do you encounter *mu*? This is the moment where breakthrough is possible; this is the moment in which we are given the opportunity to die and be reborn. Everyone has experienced such moments in their lives; perhaps some people have experienced them many times. Such situations occur every time we feel that we are facing a wall concerning some issue, and feel that we can go no further. Inevitably, what happens is that we are distracted by one or more of our six sense organs and we lose this valuable opportunity to awaken. In a Christian context, these six sense organs are seen to operate as Satan, working hard to prevent us from seeing God. It is at this point that our faith, as well as our awareness, must be strong, not allowing these interferences to succeed in deterring us on our journey. It is ultimately our strong faith, coupled with determination, that will enable us to carry through to the end.

Another crucial point to keep in mind is that we must not harbor any expectations of attaining enlightenment. We will never become enlightened if we consciously seek such a goal. Yet Zen texts are constantly emphasizing the importance of enlightenment. Is this not a contradiction? Let us look at it this way: in terms of our everyday world of appearance, the *momjit* world, we need to make distinctions, such as sentient beings and enlightened beings, right and wrong, good and bad, and so forth. If I want to go to Manhattan from Stony Brook, I must travel westward. If I go to the east, I will not arrive at my destination. If someone says he wants to go to Manhattan but he is moving eastward, I must intervene and show him the correct direction. Similarly, in the spiritual realm a medicine is needed that can help people to turn themselves around. This medicine is reflected in the term *great enlightenment* and may be followed by such directions as "sit down!" or "turn around!" or "wake up!" However, once the student's interest is aroused and he sits down with the determination to enter the invisible world of *mom*, the teacher should not continue telling him to sit down. Similarly, to use the term *enlightenment* is no longer necessary at this point. It is only used in the beginning, before one starts to practice. Once he begins to practice, he understands that in the *mom* world dualism does not exist, and thus he and "enlightenment" are inherently one with each other.

Faith and Understanding

Hua-yen philosophy, which we will discuss in more detail at a later point, states that there are four stages of spiritual development: faith, understanding, practice, and perfect enlightenment. Many people feel that understanding must precede, and not follow, faith. Is this really so? Let us look at the issue a bit more deeply. It may be true that a certain amount of intellectual understanding of the history and philosophy of Buddhism is necessary in order for one to begin to have some faith in its teachings. However, this kind of understanding will not enable one to automatically enter the door of faith. Faith is something that goes beyond mere intellectual understanding. There is a leaping stage which must first occur before one can acquire true faith; at this stage all of one's previous concepts and habitual ways of understanding are broken. This is what I have termed the "shipwreck experience"; it totally breaks apart all of one's preconceived beliefs, as I discussed earlier.

But what happens now? Is one's understanding unswerving and his knowledge fixed? Does he now have no further questions to ask? Quite the contrary: at this point, paradoxically, at the point that one acquires faith, his doubts become even greater, yet they are of a different sort. Before he acquired faith, enlightenment seemed rather remote and abstract, and not to be taken very seriously—it seemed perhaps like some faraway dream. Once faith is acquired, however, enlightenment cannot be ignored and various questions and concerns begin to arise. In Christian theology, it is said that faith seeks understanding, that is, because once you have faith, you automatically begin to have things that need to be understood and clarified.

The four-step process of faith, understanding, practice, and enlightenment, as mentioned earlier, is a basic tenet of Hua-yen philosophy. Zen, however, goes beyond such a view; in the Zen tradition, to have faith means to accept the fact of the teacher's enlightenment. It means to fully recognize the meaning of nonduality; thus I, as an ordinary, sentient being, am also an awakened, enlightened Buddha.

What about the monks and hermits who practice in isolated areas such as monasteries or forests? Should practice be a practice of nonduality, and therefore, as a reflection of that nonduality, should practitioners remain connected with the mainstream of society? It is my understanding that one's practice must always remain dualistic. My reasoning is this: once you acquire faith, you begin to see your own shortcomings as never before. Previous to one's acquiring faith, this did not matter so much, but once faith becomes firm, all of one's habitual tendencies begin to make their presence known in a very powerful way; they can no longer be ignored. Therefore, we must recognize that although the world of faith may be nondualistic (that is, not faith that I may *become* Buddha, but rather, faith that I *am* Buddha), the world of practice can only be dualistic in the sense that wrong is not right. One's dualistic habits and tendencies, although they are participants in the realm of nonduality, must be recognized and understood as also being different from that realm. The fact of their non-separation should not be further expanded to imply their complete and utter identity with their source, *mom*. Right and wrong originate from the same source, but they themselves are not the same as *mom*.

WHAT IS ENLIGHTENMENT?

I would like to begin this section by relating two stories. The first was mentioned by the sixteenth Zen master in Korea, the venerable Sosan, in his book entitled *Manual of Zen Buddhism*. He said, "It is very easy to get enlightened while doing *hwadu* meditation. How easy? As easy as touching your nose while washing your face." It is difficult *not* to touch your nose while washing your face; after all, your nose is part of your face! Therefore, the connotation is that when you meditate with the *hwadu*, enlightenment is right there with you; it is unavoidable.

The second story was told by Korean Zen master Kyung-bung, who died only about twenty years ago. He said, "If you wait to attain enlightenment until after you have exhaled, then you will never attain enlightenment." The message here is really the same as the message of the first story: enlightenment is with you right now, not at some future time.

These two stories, then, are telling us the same thing. Most people think that enlightenment happens after they meditate or by means of meditation, but this perspective involves the concept of time. The Zen masters above, and indeed all Zen masters, tell us that this way of thinking is not correct; rather, enlightenment is already with us. From these two stories we can see that attaining enlightenment requires nothing other than giving up the search for it. At the moment we stop seeking, enlightenment is there. What is enlightenment? It means returning to our original nature, that is, our *mom*, which implies being natural, like a newborn baby, having no greed, anger, or ignorance. Babies do nothing on their own in order to help others, yet just by the fact of their very being, they bring great happiness to us. Whenever a baby appears on the scene, immediately everyone feels drawn to it. Being enlightened works the same way: just by being natural, you help others. In terms of your job, you can have any kind of career. The important thing is to return to your original nature, to your *mom*. In this way, you can enjoy your own life as well as help others enjoy theirs. This is true freedom.

In academic terms, religiosity means not being selfish, self-centered, or egocentric. To pursue your own interests at the expense of others is not religiosity. If you are a great evangelist but remain egocentric, you cannot be said to be religious. One's title is not important, nor is it necessary to have an affiliation with any religious heritage.

Enlightenment, or religiosity, may also be called love or compassion. It is an egoless love, which helps others without any expectation of reward. It also implies going beyond the limitations of our artificial, man-made culture, in which the time system has gained supreme authority. A baby does not operate within a time system, nor does an enlightened person.

Because of our deeply rooted habits and ingrained conditions, such a perspective may seem daunting, to say the least. As Jesus said, ". . . to enter the kingdom of heaven is harder than for a camel to pass through the eye of a needle." He also said, "But with God, all things are possible." A Buddhist might say, "With an enlightened understanding, all things are possible." How does one attain this enlightened understanding? Buddhism traditionally emphasizes the importance of practice. This means nothing more than freeing yourself from the three poisons of greed, anger, and ignorance. When you are questioning with the *hwadu*, at that time is there any greed, anger, or ignorance? You are totally free from those poisons if you are sincere in your questioning. How religious *hwadu* meditation is! Actually getting rid of the three poisons means returning to your original nature, to *mom*. It is because of these three poisons that we have become separated from our original nature in the first place.

From a different angle, a more positive one, Buddhism espouses the three learnings, that is, keeping the precepts, practicing meditation, and obtaining wisdom. How can we keep all the many precepts prescribed by the Buddha? By meditating with the *hwadu*. The worst violation of the precepts is thought to be *ahimsa*, or killing. Are you killing anyone when you practice *hwadu* meditation? The second violation is stealing: While questioning with the *hwadu*, are you stealing anything from anyone? The third violation is sexual misconduct, the fourth is lying, and the fifth is taking intoxicants that damage your body. When you are practicing with the *hwadu*, you are keeping all these five precepts.

The most important teaching of Buddhism centers around the issue of enlightenment. The word *Buddha* itself means "enlightened one." What Buddha taught is the teaching of enlightenment. How do we understand this term and its significance for our lives? Actually, the word has several different meanings. Buddhism says it is salvation, or liberation from bondage, in particular the bondage of ignorance. It is also viewed as a flowing together with the flood of *saṃsāra*, the latter being the three poisons. Thus, it may be seen as a loss of one's individual sense of control, a loss of one's sense of separation. Ironically, through this "loss," we can be rescued from the flood of transmigration, or the endless cycle of death followed by rebirth. The word *enlightenment* may also be seen as a renunciation, or as a purification. The dictionary has several definitions for the term.

The sect of Zen Buddhism focuses primarily on people's intellectualizations, on their calculating minds. We tend to constantly make comparisons and are continuously analyzing our situations and asking, "Which way is better?" Yet such an attitude only keeps us in the dark. Rather, we should just sit and meditate.

The history of Zen is less than two thousand years old. Bodhidharma, the original founder of Zen, introduced it in China in AD 550. It then spread to Korea, Japan, and all the other Asian countries. It came to the West only very recently. In terms of the history of the universe, it is like a newborn baby. In the past, the Zen Buddhist civilization was oriented around the monastery. This is in contrast to Christian history; Christians have consistently been church-oriented. The monastery, however, is somewhat like a military school: strict guidelines, in terms of laws, rules, regulations, and so forth, are necessary in order to maintain a smoothly running operation. We need to keep in mind, though, that the essence of Zen is not bound by the monastery culture. The Zen guidelines were composed by the monks in the monastery in order to keep it operating efficiently. Thus, the monks systematized a monastery dogma. However, we must not mistake this for Zen itself. Zen lies beyond all systematization; it lies beyond all dogma.

Yet as long as we do not become attached to the Zen guidelines created by the monasteries, we can learn much from them. One of the most fundamental guidelines was related to the theory of change. All of the Zen disciplines were, in essence, based on this theory of change. It was understood that the practitioner needed to change himself, or become transformed, into a being of wisdom. For this, the guidelines, in the sense of discipline, were necessary. To elucidate their theory of change, the Zen masters borrowed stories from the external world. One example they used was water. We know that if water is cooled to a great degree, it becomes ice. Yet the reverse is also true: if it is heated up, the ice will melt. If we keep on heating it, the water will become steam, and eventually act as a cloud which can cover the entire world. Zen Buddhists use this understanding as a simile to develop their theory of transformation, the idea being that if you practice continuously, your hard karma (ice) will become melted (water). If you continue further, even that soft state will disappear and you will ascend to heaven. In that formless state, you will be able to penetrate everywhere, covering the entire universe. In Buddhism this is called *āśraya parāvṛtti*, or transformation of the basis. Again, however, it is important that we do not become attached to such an understanding, as it betrays the fundamental principle of Zen as described in the two stories mentioned at the beginning of this discussion.

Another useful story related to the theory of transformation is that of the tadpole and the frog. A tadpole has a very limited life; it can only survive in a pond. If there is no water, it will die. When it becomes a frog, however, it can jump out of the pond and live on land. It no longer has to rely on the water for its existence. Zen Buddhism tells us that we are a tadpole now, but after we attain enlightenment we will be a frog and live in complete freedom.

One more simile is that of a caterpillar and a butterfly. A caterpillar cannot survive without the leaves of a tree to chew on, but when it becomes a butterfly, it can fly away to wherever it wants.

This idea of transformation itself is limiting, as mentioned above. It was produced by those within the monastery system, but what about those of us living in the modern world? We must understand these stories symbolically and not become attached to them. Ultimately, Zen says that we do not need to transform ourselves from one state to another. Why? Because we are already enlightened beings, just as we are.

The present guidelines for Zen Buddhist practice generally embrace the three-stage theory, that is, the harmonization of the body through sitting in the lotus position, the harmonization of the breath through *t'an-t'ien* breathing, and the harmonization of the mind through *hwadu* meditation. This was discussed earlier in more depth. It must be kept in mind however, that these guideline were created many hundreds of years ago, within the context of a culture that was very different from the one in which we are now living. We need to have a clear understanding about how to interpret these guidelines. Without such an understanding, we will not be successful if we try to use them as a manual for our practice.

It is also important to realize that these guidelines developed gradually, to meet the demands of the practitioners who lived in the monasteries. However, in our modern society, the great majority of Zen practitioners do not live in a monastery. Thus, we need to revise the guidelines so that they will be appropriate for these lay practitioners. Certainly this can be seen as a very reasonable and natural demand. History is continually changing and developing; it is not like a corpse sitting somewhere in a museum. Among the many things Zen Buddhism is not, it is certainly not a museum sculpture. Although the spirit of Zen may be seen as changeless, the guidelines themselves have the ability, and in these modern times the need, to be changed. Changing the guidelines does not mean destroying the original spirit of Zen—far from it. In fact, the reverse is true in order to keep the spirit of Zen alive. We need to make this effort of revising the guidelines.

The most important thing to be changed is related to the experience of enlightenment. It is fundamental that our understanding of the enlightenment experience does not imprison it within a time system. In other words, although certain Zen masters in the past, as well as the Buddha himself, had an experience of enlightenment, this does not mean that we should strive to have such an experience in some future time and place. It is true that in a historical context we may say that the Buddha's enlightenment, as well as the enlightenment of all the Zen masters, occurred within the framework of a temporal system. Yet in all the accounts of these various enlightenment experiences, we will always find a reference to the fact that they did not occur within any time frame. This understanding is reflected very clearly in the Zen master's story about enlightenment not occurring on the exhale that follows the inhale. We must not wait for the exhale in order to become enlightened. We need not wait for anything, because enlightenment has nothing to do with past, present, or future.

In this sense, Zen Buddhist logic is completely different from a warrior's logic. President Bush says that if we invade Iraq, we can free the Iraqi people. This is a warrior's logic; it believes that if I do this, then that will follow. Zen wants to liberate us from such a logic. Zen logic has nothing to do with any futuristic goals. Rather, the Zen approach originated from such stories as the ones mentioned above, about not believing that you will be enlightened until after you exhale and that enlightenment is as easy as touching your nose while washing your face. These stories point to the immediacy of enlightenment according to Zen.

In contrast to this, many people who are interested in enlightenment see it as requiring a transformation on the part of the practitioner. Certainly we can see such a transformation occurring constantly in the animal world: a tadpole becomes a frog, and a caterpillar changes into a butterfly. The world of a tadpole is much different than that of a frog; similarly, the life of a caterpillar is vastly more limiting than that of a butterfly. These evidences of transformation provide a motivation for the practitioner: now I am a tadpole (or caterpillar), but someday I can become a frog (or butterfly).

However, the Zen stories of enlightenment being like touching your nose while washing your face and of not waiting to exhale before you attain enlightenment—these stories belie the idea of enlightenment involving a process of transformation. Yet on the other hand, we cannot say that transformation does not occur. The point to be understood here is that enlightenment and transformation do not occur as the result of our effort or our striving. When we meditate, we are doing so as enlightened beings. We already exist within the enlightened state; there is no need for us to try and "get" it. Yet again, the paradox is that this does not mean that meditation is unnecessary. We do need to meditate, but not in order to become enlightened. We simply meditate as enlightened beings.

NO NEED FOR TRANSFORMATION

The *hwadu* has been used by East Asian Buddhist practitioners for hundreds of years, and has become associated with several systems of Buddhist thought. Indeed, it has become so completely incorporated into East Asian Buddhist theory and practice that its meaning is rarely questioned or analyzed. Yet we who live in the contemporary world can only benefit from investigating this term *hwadu* more thoroughly. Practitioners in particular need to understand its real significance for their lives.

The *hwadu* is not intended to be a means by which we may attain a preconceived goal or benefit. To view it as such is to view it from a causal, or utilitarian, standpoint, in which the practitioner is seeking some type of gain, whether for himself or for others. Yet the understanding of all the enlightened Zen masters is that such an approach does not accord with the teachings of the Buddha.

Interestingly, when we look into how the monks and nuns in the majority of today's monasteries are practicing, we find that their understanding is also not in agreement with the Buddha's teachings. The main purpose of most practitioners living in Buddhist monasteries is to become enlightened. Their goal in itself stems from a causal or utilitarian viewpoint. The monk or nun is seeking some state he or she feels is lacking or absent within him or herself. This is true of the monks and nuns who live in Christian monasteries as well. Although Christians learn from an early age that God exists in all things, including humans, those who enter Christian monasteries do not necessarily feel convinced of this; rather, they are hoping to "find" God through their experience of living in the monastery. Clearly, then, there is a conflict between the primary teachings of both Buddhism and Christianity and the understanding held by many practitioners of these religions.

As discussed in the previous section, the message given to us by the two Zen masters, Sosan and Kyung-bung, can be summarized as follows: we don't need to change ourselves from a tadpole to a frog, or from a caterpillar to a butterfly, or from ice to water. Such changes reflect a kind of alchemy; they are not Buddhism. In East Asia it is believed that the sages taught a way in which iron can be changed into gold. This is an alchemical idea which emphasizes the importance of transformation. Yet what kind of transformation is being discussed here? There is a vast difference between an alchemical transformation and Buddhist transformation. This is an important point for us to realize.

If we correctly comprehend the testimony of the Zen masters, we will understand that we don't need to be transformed. The tadpole is beautiful just as it is. Let us enjoy being a tadpole. A tadpole is Buddha. To think that a tadpole must turn into a frog does not adequately reflect the spirit of Buddhism. Each of us, as we are, is already Buddha; we need not add or take away anything in order to become so. To try to become a frog is just an old, useless habit based on a greedy, utilitarian desire. If, in time, the tadpole becomes a frog, so be it. If it is going to happen, it will happen on its own. If we try to force a change, this is like a businessman trying to become a millionaire overnight.

Why do we meditate, then, if we are already Buddha? Why do we use a *hwadu*? This is a crucial question asked by many serious practitioners as well as those who are less informed. It is here that we need to understand what happens when we use the *hwadu*. It may be said that raising a question with the *hwadu*, such as, "Why did Chao-chou say 'Mu'?" is similar to St. Paul's encounter with the resurrected Jesus. For those who are not familiar with this story, it is as follows: According to St. Paul's own testimony, he went to Damascus to persecute the Christians. As an adamant Jew, he was completely unsympathetic to the Christian allegiance to Jesus as their savior and as the son of God. On the way, however, he had a vision of Jesus, who waylaid him and asked, "Why are you persecuting me and my followers?" After this deeply moving experience, Paul changed his beliefs completely, converting to Christianity and becoming a spokesperson for all its followers.

Many other Christian leaders have also claimed to have had an encounter with God. Using the *hwadu* is exactly this same kind of experience. At the very moment that the practitioner asks the question, if he is sincere in his asking, he will have no theory, no pride, no knowledge, nothing but *Mu*. He only holds the question, "What is mu? Why did Chao-chou say 'Mu'?" in his mind. The issue of enlightenment should hold no importance for him whatsoever. To have this kind of attitude in one's mind, and to sincerely maintain this kind of questioning, acts as a shock to one's system, that is, to one's physical, mental, and emotional modes of operation. Yet this is the crucial attitude that is necessary to maintain, for in doing so, all one's karmas begin to disappear. This is the moment when you are with God, or with Buddha. The shock that is produced is actually a natural response of the body, mind, and emotions; it is not a product of one's artificial effort. It may be interpreted as a type of doubt, but this doubt is not negative, and it does not destroy anything.

What we are discussing here may sound similar to the teachings of the Sōto school of Zen. Sōto practitioners advise their followers to "just sit." They say we should not expect to get enlightened, and that if we sit for one minute, we are a one-minute Buddha. Similarly, if we sit for two or three minutes, we are a two or three-minute Buddha. The message then is that we are already inherently Buddha. We need not expect any kind of special effort in order for this to be so. This sounds very much like what we are saying about using the *hwadu*: the moment that you raise the question, that is the moment you are with the Buddha, that is the moment that you are with God. This may also be called returning to our original nature. When we use the *hwadu*, we are returning to our *mom*, our original nature, which is that of a newborn baby.

What we need to emphasize here, however, is that being with God or being with Buddha should not be interpreted dualistically. Many people hold onto preconceived understandings or beliefs, which they have maintained for so many years or even lifetimes. They may interrupt their questioning with some doubt, such as, "Am I really returning to God?" Or they may believe: "I am still a sentient being, but if I can become enlightened, then I can be a Buddha. Then all my problems will be solved." This is a dualistic attitude.

We need to realize that all of these emotions—skepticism, doubt, even hope—are functions of the Buddha. The Buddha knows everything; we need to let him go about his business. If we have an urgent problem in our lives, we need to attend to it. That's fine—but later, when we have time, we should return to our *hwadu* questioning. Karmically, our dualistic behavior will be weakened by such practice. Gradually, we will be able to experience each of the fifty-two stages of practice, as outlined by the Hua-yen teachings. Along the way, we are performing Buddha's job. If we want to adopt certain techniques, such as breath control, yoga, tai chi, and so forth, that is no problem. Certainly it does no harm to make use of such practices. Yet as *hwadu* practitioners we must inevitably return to the *hwadu*. No matter what our outer circumstances may be, as practitioners we are always living in the world of the *hwadu*. It becomes a part of us; no separation will be seen or experienced.

ATTAINING SALVATION?

Many years ago I was involved in a rather frightening mishap. I was standing at the edge of a cliff on a mountainside, gazing with awe and wonder at the beautiful scenery in front of me. Engaged as I was in this rapturous experience, I paid no attention to where I was standing. Without thinking, I stepped out into the space beyond the cliff. Naturally, I fell off the cliff, my body hurtling through space, and then I crashed to the ground with a jolt. The distance from the top of the cliff, where I had been standing, to the ground below was about three stories, certainly enough to cause great injury, if not death. Fortunately, I suffered no serious injuries, although I was emotionally quite shaken. During the time that I was falling, no thoughts entered my head except for the awareness of the catastrophic event that was happening along with an overwhelming fear concerning my impending fate. I truly felt that I was about to meet my death.

After that incident occurred, I thought about it quite a bit, asking myself this question: As I was falling, before I hit the ground, was there a chance for me to be saved? Right there, during those agonizing moments, could I have possibly attained enlightenment? Later, I amended my question to this: Supposing I had died from my fall and was just a lifeless corpse lying there on the ground: could I have been saved even then?

Intellectually speaking, there was nothing I could have done to become saved at that point. Any intellectual person would probably remark, "Of course you couldn't be saved. You were already dead. Even while you were falling, before you hit the ground, it would have been impossible to achieve your salvation; your thoughts would have been entirely preoccupied with your fear about what was happening." Indeed, one of my colleagues replied, when I asked him this question, "Too late!" A deeply religious person may have had a different understanding of the matter, however. Such a person, having maintained a consistent spiritual practice for many years and thus having been accustomed to embodying the unified consciousness that reflects such a practice, may very well have been able to possess the awareness that whatever the outcome of such a disaster as falling off a cliff, he/she had nothing to fear.

However, I have in mind not such a deeply religious person, but rather an ordinary sentient being like myself, one who does not necessarily live a life devoted to consistent spiritual practice. For such a person, is salvation possible while falling off a cliff? Is salvation possible after his death, while he lies as a corpse on the ground? After pondering this issue deeply, I have come to the following conclusion regarding both questions: yes, that person can be saved. In fact, that word *become* is misleading, because in fact that person is already saved.

In Buddhism, the relevant and powerful statements concerning the issue of salvation are the following: "You are Buddha." "I am Buddha." "Everyone is Buddha." "All sentient beings are Buddha." The phrase "sentient being" is all-inclusive, referring not only to people but to all phenomena, such as rocks, plants, furniture, houses, places, and so forth. Every sentient being is said to contain the Buddha-nature, which means that every sentient being is already saved, just by his/her/its very nature.

What does it mean to be saved? Basically, I would say that it means that I, or you, or anyone/anything else, do not exist as a separate, independent entity, but am included as a part of the essence of all other sentient beings. There is a famous poem by the Japanese monk Uicheon, who lived during the twelfth century, that states: "In a speck of dust, the entire world is completely contained." Uicheon is saying here that this one tiny speck of dust is actually all-encompassing; it embraces everything that exists in the entire universe. Similarly, to say "I am Buddha" means that I, too, contain within myself the entire world. Every moment, whether past, present, or future, wherever I am, no matter what the situation or condition, I am Buddha, I embody the entire universe within myself. As such, I exist beyond the limits of time and space. Thus, before I fell from the cliff, during my fall from the cliff, after I hit the ground, as I lay lifeless on the ground—no matter what my physical state or condition, I am Buddha, I am saved.

Many so-called religious people are unknowingly misled by the sectarian dogma being proclaimed by their religious leaders. This unfortunate situation exists within the confines of any organized religion, be it Christianity or Buddhism or Islam or Judaism or Hinduism or whatever. Just to give one example: if a Buddhist falling off a cliff prays to Kwan Yin (the bodhisattva who promises to save all sentient beings) while falling, he/she is adhering to a certain Buddhist dogma. The word *God* has always held a profound meaning for people of most civilizations. We believe that God has the power to save us, whether we be rich or poor, intelligent or illiterate, good or evil. Jesus Christ has said, "I come for the sinner, for the lost lamb." We grasp onto these statements and beliefs, hoping and praying that they are true. Yet the teachings of Zen Buddhism tell us emphatically that all of us, whether alive or dead, healthy or sick, are already saved. We need to look at this question of what it really means to be saved. We tend to view salvation on our own terms, due to our ignorance (about the "future") and our greed (which is a product of our fear, again about the "future"). Yet this attitude reflects a lack of faith. What is faith? Seen from a different vantage point than that discussed earlier, we may say that it is nothing more than the ability, or rather the willingness, to return to the Buddha, to return to God. What this means is that we must view the world, and ourselves, from God's point of view, and not from our own limited understanding. We need to see the larger picture and hold onto the position held by God. It is only then that we will be seeing the world, and ourselves, correctly. We need to let God, or Buddha, speak, think, and act through us. This is the true meaning of faith.

Salvation has generally been discussed as if it were a material commodity, that is, as something to be achieved or acquired. From this basic misunderstanding, many misinformed theories have been generated, such as, "If I do this, I can be saved," or "If I meditate for ten years, I can become enlightened." There has been an ongoing debate in East Asian Buddhist circles concerning how enlightenment is attained. Is it sudden, that is, occurring instantaneously, in a flash, or is it gradual, thus ripening into awakening after a lengthy period of practice? However, this issue of sudden or gradual is not the fundamental question to be raised. Rather, we need to inquire: What is the nature of enlightenment? What does it mean to be enlightened, to attain salvation? The debate over sudden versus gradual is largely a debate about causation. Yet East Asian Buddhism teaches that cause is effect; the two are intertwined and cannot be separated. This truth brings us back full circle to the previous statement: salvation means that we recognize that we are already whole, that we are an ongoing part of the universe, and are not in any way separate from it. We already *are* what we are seeking. Meister Eckhart, the noted German theologian of the late thirteenth century, stated, "The eye with which I see God is the same eye with which God sees me." Our salvation is already, inherently, accomplished. Let's open our eyes and our minds and see that truth, and not allow ourselves to be prey to dogmas that are based on hope or fear. Let us be willing to return to God, to Buddha. When we do so, we can realize for ourselves our own innate identity as enlightened beings.

THE STRANGE BEHAVIOR OF ZEN MASTERS:
BEATINGS AND SHOUTINGS

What happens when a practitioner begins to question with the *hwadu*? With regard to the *hwadu mu* as described earlier, there are two possible responses that a practitioner can have with regard to Chao-chou's statement of denial. The first is that of utter astonishment. The questioner expects a positive reply: "Of course a dog has the Buddha-nature!" The expectation, both consciously and unconsciously, is that the answer will be "Yes!" So when Chao-chou says "No," the questioner is left with a tremendous feeling of bewilderment.

The second possible reaction to Chao-chou's reply is that of doubt, followed by an analytical investigation. This is the response of an intellectual; he will immediately begin to ponder the matter, trying to figure out the reason why Chao-chou said, "*Mu!*" He will attack the problem again and again from his own limited mental perspective, attempting with all his might to understand the rationale behind Chao-chou's response.

Of course, there is a third possible reaction, that of a nonbeliever, who on hearing Chao-chou's answer, will simply abandon his practice altogether, feeling that the teacher has no ability to help him in his spiritual quest.

The Zen master who is interested in enabling his students to attain awakening will be primarily concerned with the practitioner who exhibits the second type of response, that is, the one who questions the issue mentally. The third type has no interest in pursing a relationship with the master and the first type does not need the master's help at this point. This first type has already begun the process of working on the *hwadu* correctly. He does not mentally doubt Chao-chou's answer, but merely wonders at it. With continued faith and perseverance, he may eventually break through to awakening. The second type, however, the intellectual, needs the help of the Zen master, and this is where the latter's beatings and shoutings can be very useful.

This second type of practitioner has arrived at an impasse in his practice. He has accumulated a vast amount of knowledge throughout the course of his life, and he has become extremely skillful at manipulating this knowledge. For him, the various Buddhist doctrines and theories are not an effective means of dismantling his knowledge; it is too deeply embedded. Only such irrational tactics such as beatings and shoutings may accomplish the aim of breaking up his deep-rooted attachments to his mental world. Certainly the linguistic statements used by the teacher will serve no purpose, for this type of practitioner will merely translate them according to his preconceived way of thinking and begin to analyze them in that way. This is not Zen, however. In Zen, the aim is to get the student to completely abandon all such mental concepts and fixations so that he can view the world with new eyes. Thus, any kind of rational, linguistic approach on his part will be instantly vetoed by the teacher.

Whatever the student says, the teacher will say, "No." The beatings and shoutings used by the teacher are essentially symbolic gestures which represent this "No." The internal message given is continually, "No." The beatings and shoutings work like a bomb, destroying all of the intellectual hiding places that have been created and maintained by the student throughout his life.

There are various other perspectives through which we may understand the use of beatings and shoutings by a Zen master. One of these perspectives is that of nondualism. It is very difficult for a spiritual teacher to be of help to a student who is heavily armed with dualistic dogma. One way for the teacher to break through this dualism is through the use of beatings and shoutings. When the teacher beats the student, the body is attacked but the real target is dualism. By striking the body of the practitioner, the teacher attacks, and ultimately defeats, the practitioner's dualistic way of thinking.

It may also be seen that the Zen master's beatings and shoutings enable the practitioner to break free from his attachment to a causal way of thinking. Many students of Buddhism unwittingly fall into a causal approach to practice, believing that meditation is a means to enlightenment. They entertain the hope that by meditating they can transform their ignorance into wisdom. However, if they are meditating with this aim, this is not true meditation according to Zen. Many Zen monks think that using a *hwadu* is a way to help them achieve their goal. This way of thinking represents a modern tragedy for the religious world. A similar attitude may be seen in the Christian realm: prayer is viewed as a means to obtain God's mercy. Neo-Confucians as well are attached to such a causal system, believing that respect for others may help one to become a sage. This, however, was not the original message of Confucius. These types of causal beliefs can be effectively destroyed by the Zen master's beatings and shoutings.

The time system, which is a preconceived, man-made system, may also be dismantled through the beatings and shoutings of a skilled Zen master. Ordinarily, human beings function within the framework of a time system. We all think in terms of past, present, and future; this is universal. Yet we have become imprisoned within this system; it has completely overtaken our lives to the point that we are ruled by it. Although in the mundane world such a system may be effective, in terms of the religious world, our reliance on it prevents us from realizing the fundamental truth of nonduality. This, again, is where the beatings and shoutings of the Zen master may be useful. They can help break apart our time-oriented views so that we may see things from a new, transformed awareness. Our intellectual fortress can be completely torn down; it is at this point that we may truly be called religious practitioners.

In these modern times, however, the fortress of the mind is often affirmed, supported, and encouraged to grow. The Zen approach is different. It seeks to completely eliminate such a defense system. It enables the practitioner to abandon his rational way of thinking altogether. This may be most easily accomplished through the beatings and shoutings of the Zen master.

PROBLEMS IN PRACTICE

I have read many articles recently, and have had quite a few discussions with various knowledgeable people as well, regarding the topic of *hwadu* meditation. What I have observed from my readings and discussions is that people's opinions about the *hwadu* fall into two distinct categories: "pro" and "con." Those in the "pro" category feel that the *hwadu* is the only means by which enlightenment can be achieved, whereas those in the "con" category feel that the use of the *hwadu* is ineffective. However, from my observation, I have noticed that both sides are experiencing a sense of crisis regarding the proper use of *hwadu* meditation. I feel that the suffering on both sides is intensifying: I hear it as a scream for help, and I cannot ignore these screams. I will now look at each side in more detail.

The message of the "pro" people is simple: using *hwadu* is the only way to become enlightened. However, these people realize that many, if not most, people are not practicing it correctly. People may appear to be using *hwadu* during their meditation but in reality they are not. This is the crux of the crisis. In order to help these people, the "pros" continue to emphasize the teachings of the ancient Zen masters, reminding them of the basic fact of nonduality and so forth. Some of the "pro" people have proposed to develop some kind of special technique of meditation in order to help those who are having difficulties, such as putting earplugs in their ears or having them listen to tranquilizing music with headphones, and so forth. However, such methods are not a solution, as they only serve to increase a sense of duality between the practitioner and the practice. In my opinion, the problem is that practitioners are not examining themselves deeply. In other words, they lack the necessary practice of brutal and honest self-criticism.

When I observe the "con" people, I see that they can be further divided into two groups. The first group consists of people who have tried using the *hwadu*, but feel that it doesn't work, so they give up and claim that it cannot lead to enlightenment. These people, I feel, are innocent in the sense that they are not aiming to malign or demean others; they simply feel that the *hwadu* has no value. The second group is more sophisticated. These people are intellectually well armed: they have much knowledge, having by and large been trained or at least influenced by modern scholars. Of course, there are many things to be learned from their research, yet what I feel is lacking in their comments is any real interest in Zen meditation. They have no deep desire for spiritual practice. They are isolating themselves within their fortress of intellectual security, and from there they feel safe enough to freely attack others. Again, as with the "pro's," I feel that there is an absence of brutal self-criticism. In a way, these people cannot be blamed entirely for their views. The media is forcing them to feel as they do, for the media sees any true spiritual practice, that is, any practice based on nondualism, as mysticism, and looks at it with a skeptical and disdainful eye. But putting blame aside, I find that there is presently no room in the consciousness of the "con" people to accept the mission of the *hwadu*. What is the mission? It is, metaphorically speaking, to cause the practitioner to have an experience of being in a shipwreck, as I discussed earlier. Most of the "con" people are simply not ready for such an experience. They have not reached the point in their lives at which they are able to accept the possibility of, or the need for, any real or fundamental change in the way they view things.

The Nature of the Problem

Two facts need to be mentioned here: one concerning spirituality in general and one concerning *hwadu* meditation specifically. First of all, in Korea today, and indeed all over the world, an increasing spiritual thirst is becoming more and more evident among people of all ages and from all sectors. We are all experiencing the pressures caused by our modern way of living and are searching for ways to alleviate these stresses. As a result, we are discovering and learning about various techniques that can presumably enable us to calm our minds and/or strengthen our bodies. Some of these techniques include tai chi, yoga, and chi kung, as well as various forms of breathing exercises and meditation. Any and all of these techniques are certainly capable of helping us to feel better.

The second fact that needs to be recognized is that *hwadu* meditation is, by its very nature, not intended to alleviate people's tensions and stress. Its practice is far too serious and demanding for it to be categorized among the previously mentioned methods that are on the market today. This is important for people to realize so that they don't attempt to compare *hwadu* meditation with any of these other methods, and so that they don't hold any false illusions or expectations about either the purpose or the value of the *hwadu*. It requires tremendous discipline and diligence.

It is also helpful to remember that the *hwadu* method of meditation was introduced and practiced by Zen masters many hundreds of years ago, when the economy of the country, whether it was Korea, China, Japan, or any other country, was completely self-supported. If food was needed, people went into the fields and planted rice and vegetables. If fuel was needed, they went into the mountains and collected firewood. In such an atmosphere of relative simplicity, using the *hwadu* was undoubtedly much easier than it is in today's world. The most vital requirement for *hwadu* meditation is the ability to attain a state of total concentration, so that one can then transcend the limits of time and space. In our modern society, to reach such a state is not an easy task, as we are constantly being bombarded by all kinds of external distractions wherever we go. We cannot even try to escape them at home, as most of us now own television sets, radios, computers, telephones, and numerous other technological gadgets.

Another important feature of the *hwadu* is that it is not intended to be practiced only during the time of one's formal sitting meditation. Rather, it is supposed to be used during each and every one of our four possible bodily positions: sitting, standing, lying, and walking. In other words, regardless of one's physical situation, whether he/she is in the meditation hall, the garden, the kitchen, the car, the store, the office, or wherever, his/her mind should be with the *hwadu*. Is it possible for modern people to maintain such total, uninterrupted concentration?

It was in order to alleviate the problem of being distracted by external stimuli that serious practitioners left home in the past, and still do so today, to become monks or solitaries. They left the secular world behind and completely isolated themselves in the monastery or the mountains, living like hermits in partial or complete solitude. Yet the Zen masters taught that such an attitude, that is, of attempting to avoid difficult external conditions, was not correct. They constantly emphasized that *hwadu* meditation could be practiced by anyone, no matter who that person was or where that person lived. Many Zen practitioners living in our world today, however, have abandoned the *hwadu* method of meditation altogether, replacing it with other, easier styles of meditation, such as those mentioned earlier. Feeling the stresses of modern-day society, they have opted for practices that help to calm their minds so that they feel able to cope with all their tensions. Yet this is not the true purpose of Zen.

What is to be done? In the Chogye order, here in Korea, the leaders are in a bit of a dilemma, as they have lost a large part of their membership to these popular styles of spiritual practice. To point out the dangers of this modern trend, a group of reformers has recently arisen and become quite vocal. This group is concerned about what they view as the misbehavior and even the corruption of the religious community. They have made it a point to analyze the psychology of *hwadu* meditation, and they claim that the leaders of the Zen community, that is, the Zen teachers practicing today, are misleading people. What is the nature of their accusation? These reformists claim that the Zen leaders are "sugar-coating" *hwadu* practice by promising that if done correctly it leads one to enlightenment. The reformers point out that this was never the Buddha's message. According to Mahāyāna understanding, the Buddha intended for us know that we are all already enlightened, just as we are. So how can practicing the *hwadu* with such a futuristic goal in mind ever produce the correct results?

The majority of practitioners, however, are seduced by these promises of enlightenment. They don't believe that they are already enlightened. They don't understand that their real task is to awaken to their inherent essence as fully enlightened beings. They believe instead that by donating money or medicine or by providing gifts to the monks and leaders of their order they can earn merit and thus eventually gain salvation. The leaders in turn are monetarily benefiting from such attitudes, as they are the recipients of all these donations and gifts. Therefore, they are often reluctant to make any changes to this system. They continue to receive gifts while the members continue to practice incorrectly.

To summarize what has been said so far: (1) In the present world, *hwadu* practice is generally viewed by most people as too difficult to undertake; and (2) The leaders and monks are not willing to correct people's views, as they continue to profit from them.

The Real Meaning of Hwadu

Almost all Zen texts contain at least some discussion about the use of the *hwadu* in one's practice. Indeed, *hwadu* meditation is and always has been considered the core of Zen practice. Yet this term *hwadu* is not being understood correctly by the vast majority of people living in Korea today. In my opinion, they have "stolen" the term and given it a completely erroneous meaning, which translates into English as "an agenda to be pursued or an issue to be clarified." Korean journalists, politicians, and others from all walks of life use this term in their writings and/or speech freely, saying for example, "The *hwadu* of the president in this situation is . . ." or "What is the *hwadu* to be discussed here?" Such uses of this term are totally incorrect; the word is currently being presented in a secular manner, but that was not the original intention of the Zen masters who first taught with it.

A similar situation may be seen to exist in the contemporary Christian world. The word *God* has also lost its original meaning, except to a very rare few. Most people these days view God as a kind of broker or agent to whom they can appeal when they have a need to be met. Yet this was certainly not the understanding of Abraham or Moses or Jesus.

Throughout the course of history humans have invented many such sacred words, whose original meaning has either been completely distorted or else has disappeared altogether. To name a few: *tao* in Taoism (meaning the Way), *ren* in Confucianism (meaning benevolence), *t'i-yung* in early Chinese thought (meaning essence-function), and so forth. The meaning of these words was originally pure and essential, but as time passed people did not practice according to the original message of the meaning, and so these terms eventually lost their power. This is a great tragedy that has occurred to our human civilization, and it explains why I say that the meaning of *hwadu* has been stolen. It no longer exists in its pure form.

In Korea, during the Koryo dynasty (from the tenth to the fourteenth century), there was a very popular event that used to occur regularly: Buddhist practitioners would gather together, not in a temple or monastery, but in a large field. There they would discuss and practice the teachings of the Buddha. As there were no boundaries to the field, anyone could attend. Such gatherings were called *yadan pŏpsŭk*, which means "Dharma seat in the wild field." Later, the Koryo was replaced by the Choson dynasty, which embraced neo-Confucianism, and this popular practice disappeared. To this day, the term *yadan pŏpsŭk* is still in use, but just like the word *hwadu*, its meaning has become greatly distorted: now when people use the term, they use it to mean "noisy." This is yet another example of a sacred term whose original meaning has been lost due to people's inability to live up to it.

So what is the original meaning of *hwadu*, the meaning reflected by the teachings of the ancient Zen masters? In my understanding, *hwadu* helps us to return to the Buddha, to the world of *mom*. The *hwadu* may be used to guide us in this journey back to the source. In the history of religion, such a message has always been the core principle: return to the Buddha, return to God, return to Allah, return to Brahma, and so forth. The special message that lies hidden within all these religions is that this source exists within each and every one of us. We ourselves contain or reflect the source that we are seeking. In the East Asian Buddhist tradition, when the ancient Zen masters saw that the practitioners did not understand or did not accept this truth, and instead viewed themselves as existing apart from their own, innate Buddha-nature, these Zen masters became angry and hit the seekers with a stick to wake them up. Parents often exhibit the same behavior, scolding or even hitting their children if they see them doing something wrong. The Zen masters recognized the severity of the practitioners' error in understanding, and wanted to help them rectify it. What was the mistake the seekers were making? In the Zen masters' eyes, the aspirants' fundamental error was that they were too attached to the scriptures. After reading a particular text, they would organize various dogmas based on their understanding and would then become imprisoned in their own dogmas. The Zen masters knew very well that this was not in accordance with Buddhist teachings. They knew that no matter how well an aspirant might understand a scripture intellectually, if he remained attached to the idea that he was not a Buddha, his understanding would yield no results, like a farmer without a harvest. So the message of the Zen masters was always the same: Don't go in the wrong direction. Return to the Buddha.

How did the use of the *hwadu* come into being? At an early stage in the history of Zen Buddhism, there emerged a division into two schools, each practicing quite differently. One school is called *Sōto* in Japanese; in Korean it is called *mukjo*. Westerners usually translate this term as "sitting only," and interpret it to imply the absence of the use of the *hwadu*. Yet if we analyze this word *mukjo*, we find that it may be broken down into two parts: *muk*, which means "silence," and *jo*, which means "bright illustration." In the *mukjo* school, then, the practice involved first quieting the mind and body and then observing the manifestation of one's field of consciousness. There are several other terms that are now in use that reflect a similar practice: they are *śamatha/vipaśyanā* in Sanskrit, *chih/kuan* in Chinese, *ting/hui* in Chinese, and *dhyāna/prajñā* in Sanskrit. These terms all have similar meanings. Yoshito Hakeda, in his commentary on the well-known Mahāyāna text entitled *The Awakening of Faith*, has translated *śamatha/vipaśyanā* as "cessation/clear observation." Chinul, whose teachings we will discuss in a later chapter, made extensive use of the combined practice of *dhyāna* (meditation) and *prajñā* (wisdom) which, again, conveys a similar meaning to *mukjo*.

The second school of Zen was called Rinzai in Japanese. This school used the *hwadu* exclusively. The Zen masters of this school observed the practitioners of the Sōto school with a critical eye and concluded that their practice was ineffective. They felt that too many seekers were using the *mukjo* practice in the hopes that someday all of their problems would be magically solved. They saw that the aspirants did not understand the true relationship between *muk* and *jo*, which is based on nonduality or nonseparation. Instead, they were striving to create a balance between the two and thus were attempting to control their practice through the use of their intellects. The Zen masters knew, however, that in order for enlightenment to occur, the intellect must be abandoned. Yet instead what was happening was that the practitioners were holding onto their intellects with all their might! It is for this reason that the Zen masters created the *hwadu*; it was used as a means to help the practitioners loosen and ultimately break their bondage to their intellect. This is always the reason why Zen masters would hit meditators with a stick. The stick itself was a *hwadu*. It helped the seeker let go of his habitual conceptual tendencies.

With reference to the techniques of the Sōto school, however, please do not misunderstand what I say. There is nothing wrong with the practice of *mukjo* if it is performed correctly. It must be understood, though, that the two aspects, *muk* and *jo*, should not be viewed as two different types of practice to be pursued. The truth of the matter is that if the first aspect, *muk*, is performed with the correct understanding, the second aspect, *jo*, will occur naturally on its own. Thus, if cessation is practiced correctly, then clear observation will automatically emerge, with no effort required on the part of the practitioner. We may see a similar truth if we look at the relationship between the sun and the clouds. When the clouds disappear, the sun is automatically seen. It doesn't have to be coaxed out in order to manifest itself; it is already there. The Zen masters, then, introduced the use of the *hwadu* in order to help the practitioner dispel the clouds, which are a reflection of his own ego, his own intellect, so that he could see the sun, or his own Buddha-nature, shining in all its beauty and magnificence.

We live in a pluralistic world; there is no way of life or culture that exists to the exclusion of all the others. The same may be said of religions, beliefs, and practices. We need to respect all views, whether it is belief in the Pure Land, use of a mantra, practice of prostration, or the performance of various types of breathing exercises. What these practitioners need to be aware of, however, is that they are all practicing *muk* or cessation. That is, these practices are all examples of the first aspect of the Sōto school practice, which involves the calming of the mind. They need to ask themselves if they are practicing it correctly. If they are, then the second part, *jo* or clear observation, will arise spontaneously. What does it mean to practice correctly? It means to break apart the whole of the intellect, the ego, and to abandon the dualism between the practice and the one who is practicing. If the seeker is able to practice in this way, then he will be in accordance with the Zen masters' original message. This has been the basic teaching of all religious saviors of the past, and remains the most vital point which all monastery leaders should be imparting to their members.

Let us now delve into the nature of the *hwadu* a little more deeply. Why is it that the *hwadu* is considered by many as being too difficult to practice? Is it merely due to the fact that it requires one's utmost concentration and discipline, as mentioned earlier? In my view, the issue goes deeper than that. In my understanding, as I mentioned earlier, the core of the nature of the *hwadu* is that it gives the practitioner the experience of being in a shipwreck. In other words, his very foundation is completely destroyed. Such an experience may be compared to an earthquake. About thirty years ago a severe earthquake struck Berkeley, California, where I was living as a graduate student. The experience was totally devastating. Inside my living quarters pictures fell off the walls and books, tables, chairs, and all the furniture were turned over. Outside in the streets, buildings collapsed and cars were demolished due to the debris that fell on them. Our lives are based on the belief that our physical foundation, the earth, is solid. When this earthquake occurred, however, this belief was completely turned around 180 degrees in my mind. Our earth is not a permanent fixture, I now realized; it can be disrupted at any time.

It is understandable that people seek security, both physical and psychological. Living in fear can and does cause many internal as well as external problems. Thus, we will do everything we can to avoid any fears that arise regarding our own mental and personal safety. Let it be understood: the *hwadu* will shake our very foundation, just as the earthquake shook my living space. What is the nature of this shipwreck, this earthquake that occurs within us as we practice the *hwadu*? What is it inside of us that is being shaken to the core?

Unlike the physical shaking of the earth caused by an earthquake, when we are shaken by the *hwadu*, it is our very belief systems, which have been developing within us from the time we are born, that are being attacked. These belief systems, which include our worldview as well as our views about ourselves, have been created by the letter culture in which we live. By letter culture I mean the value systems that we have created over hundreds and thousands of years by means of the written word. This letter culture has gone a long way to contribute to our illusion of safety; it has become a dogma for most of us, deceiving us by pretending to insulate us from fear and by claiming to make us feel strong and secure. It is like living inside a dark fortress.

The *hwadu*, however, bombs this fortress. It rips away any and all illusions we may have regarding who we are and what this world is. It does not allow us to receive the benefits that other types of meditation or spiritual practice may offer us, such as better health, ease of tensions, calmer minds, and so forth. Thus, if a teacher asserts that *hwadu* meditation can be used to achieve any such beneficial effects, he is being dishonest. We must never propagate the belief that the *hwadu* can be used in order to bring about any enhanced state of being, including enlightenment. To do so is to use the *hwadu* as a type of bait in order to lure or entice the practitioner, like an advertisement in which one says, "Use the *hwadu* and be cured!" Such tactics are greatly misleading and do not support the teachings of either the Buddha or the ancient Zen masters.

The Solution

As mentioned above, almost every East Asian Buddhist monastery these days teaches various forms of meditation in addition to the *hwadu*. Also, many universities now include Zen Buddhism among their course offerings. In Korea alone, there are about one hundred large-scale universities, most of which offer such courses, which generally include information on how to practice meditation. How are they teaching *hwadu* meditation? If we examine the Zen texts being used in these university courses and in the monasteries as well, we discover that there exists a serious problem: the texts, by and large, are based on ordinary logic as opposed to Zen logic. What is the difference between the two? In ordinary logic, a friend is a friend and an enemy is an enemy. In Zen logic, however, a friend may be an enemy and an enemy a friend. In other words, the reality of a situation and indeed, the reality of existence, cannot be based on one's preconceived understanding alone. This is a fundamental fact that Zen students need to keep in mind at all times. Yet these texts are often using ordinary people's logic, based on the intellect, in their attempts to interpret Zen logic. This is a serious mistake. The students are being misled and are thus bound to develop an incorrect understanding of the true meaning of Zen.

What is Zen logic? It is the logic of *mom*; in other words, Zen logic is primarily concerned with the entire body or essence of any phenomenon or circumstance. It thus transcends the dualism of the intellect. Ordinary logic, on the other hand, is *momjit* logic, and reflects our usual, day-to-day way of viewing ourselves and life in general. This logic, stemming from our intellect, is based entirely on dualistic concepts of good and bad, right and wrong, and so forth.

We can find many examples of Zen logic in the Buddhist texts. For example, after the Buddha gave his famous sermon on the four noble truths, one of his disciples, Kondanna, remarked that the second noble truth, which identifies desire as the cause of suffering, was in essence identical to the third noble truth, which refers to the cessation of desire. By his statement, Kondanna was using Zen logic; he was saying that the arising of a state and its cessation are no different. In other words, in one is contained the other and vice versa; they cannot be separated. In the field of science, we may discover a similar truth when we examine the law of gravity. What goes up must come down; one cannot exist without the other. This type of understanding is what we usually fail to recognize when we use our ordinary, conceptual way of thinking to view our world or ourselves.

Another example of Zen logic may be found in the Mahāyāna text mentioned earlier entitled *The Awakening of Mahāyāna Faith*, which we will discuss later in more detail. This treatise categorizes all phenomena, including all sentient beings as well as our thoughts and actions, as operating within the confines of four distinct sequential stages: (1) arising, (2) abiding (or lasting), (3) decaying, and (4) dying. The stage of arising corresponds to our physical birth; then for the major part of our lives we exist in the abiding stage; later, in old age, our bodies begin to decay; finally, at the end of our life, we die. The same process occurs with our every thought and action as well: they arise, experience a period of lasting or abiding, eventually begin to ebb or die out, and finally they disappear altogether.

For ordinary people such as you and I, these four stages are experienced as completely distinct and separate phases of a process. Usually, for most of us, it is not until a thought has already disappeared that we even realize that we were thinking the thought. Buddhist practitioners who have a slightly higher level of awareness, for example the level of a Hīnayāna Buddhist, are able to realize the existence of their thoughts when they are still at the third level, that is, before they have disappeared from their consciousness. A bodhi-sattva, who functions at an even higher level, is able to be aware of his thoughts while they are at the second stage of abiding. This is the stage at which our thoughts are most powerful; we can see the value of being able to thus catch hold of our thoughts before they begin to lose their force and die out. Only an enlightened being, a Buddha, is able to perceive his thoughts at the very moment of their inception, as they are being created in his mind. Indeed, ultimate enlightenment entails knowing right from the start exactly what is occurring within your own mind.

The crucial point that the text makes is that these four stages are said to occur simultaneously. This is a clear example of Zen logic. Everything is seen to happen right at the very beginning; there is no sequential development of one stage occurring before or after another. This understanding is also reflected in the often-quoted analogy of the water and the wave. Each is a part of the other, and they both exist together and at the same time. It is not possible to separate them into two independent entities. Similarly, *mom* and *momjit* also operate in unison. Every *mom* is also a *momjit* and every *momjit* is also a *mom*, as discussed previously.

The teachings of Hua-yen Buddhism are yet another example of this fundamental Zen truth. According to this school of thought, there exist fifty-two stages with regard to the attainment of enlightenment. The first stage refers to the arising of the desire for bodhicitta, or the wisdom mind, which reflects one's initial desire for enlightenment. Each stage represents one step farther along on the path, and the fifty-second and final stage is the attainment of ultimate enlighten-ment itself. Hua-yen thought teaches that at the moment one enters the first stage, that is, the moment when aspiration for enlightenment arises, at that very moment the last stage is inherently included. This is the timeless perspective; in theistic language, we may call it God's perspective.

It is extremely difficult to comprehend the Zen logic described above. Our intellect alone cannot accomplish such a feat, for this logic points to an understanding that lies beyond the realm of our reason. It is here that faith is required in order to bridge the gap; otherwise, the practitioner may easily be tempted to give up his practice alto-gether. If the practitioner can develop and maintain an attitude of firm conviction within himself, then eventually his intellect will soften its grip and he may catch a glimpse of the truth of nonduality.

Many, if not most, scholars, including Hakeda in his discussion of the four stages of phenomena as mentioned above (see pages 45–46 in his translation and commentary on *The Awakening of Faith*), fail to recognize the crucial need for faith on the part of the practitioner. They discuss nonduality in a straightforward, scientific manner, but do not understand that such an approach is incomplete. Something more is needed if one is to grasp the truth of the Buddha; something more is required if we are to transcend the limits of our intellect. In my opinion, it is the underlying background of faith, or the ultimate trust that we, too, are Buddha, that enables us to "cross to the other shore" and attain our goal of enlightenment. It is this issue, the issue of faith, that scholars need to recognize and address if they are to correctly and successfully interpret and communicate the Buddha's understanding.

What is the *hwadu*? It is nothing but returning to the Buddha. We must not fall prey to the temptation of mysticizing it by saying that it promises enlightenment. The *hwadu*, in and of itself, does not promise us anything. It merely points to what already is, to what exists right in front of us. If a Zen master is asked, "What is the essence of the Buddhist message?" he might reply, "Flowers are red and leaves are green" or "My nose is vertical and my eyes are horizontal."

How did the mystification of the *hwadu* arise? Whatever the answer to that question may be, we must not view the *hwadu* in such an illusory sense. The *hwadu* means to return to our ordinary, every-day life as it is. There is no mystery about it; therefore, we shouldn't try to add anything extra. Nor should we be concerned if others use different methods of practice—these things are not important. What is important is that we return to the Buddha. How can we do this? We need to eliminate our false techniques. We are already Buddha; we exist as timeless beings, as *mom*. As practitioners, we should not use *momjit* language or ways of thinking in our spiritual practice. We must move, act, think, and speak as that which we are. The *hwadu* shows us who we are: enlightenment itself. We need to wake up and celebrate our true identity.

THE NATURE OF DEATH

For a long time I held the view that an enlightened person could control the time and circumstances of his own physical death. I had read about the events surrounding Chinul's death, in which he knew one morning that he would die later that same day. He gathered his students around him and told them the news, and at the appointed time he simply sat upright in the lotus position and passed away. This story impressed me greatly. I felt that Chinul had died a perfect death and that all other deaths were but shallow, meaningless affairs. I fantasized that my own death would somehow be modeled after that of Chinul.

Several years ago, after witnessing the death of several close members of my family, I began to realize how wrong I was. I saw these people suffering in the hospital rooms and at home; they all were experiencing great pain, both physically and emotionally, yet none of them wanted to die. I observed the depth of their suffering and I began to believe that all deaths are perfect and sacred; none is less noble or profound than any other.

An event that occurred around this time also helped me to understand the holy nature of death. I was visiting in Korea and had given a lecture in which I discussed the "great death" as performed by certain Zen masters, Chinul among them. I made the statement that most people, in comparison, die a "dog's death." In Korea, this is a very derogatory term, meaning that an ordinary person's death is a somewhat shameful and pitiful affair. A woman came up to me after the lecture and questioned my statements. She said she wasn't disagreeing with me—in fact, she held the same view—but she sought further clarification on the issue. Somehow, hearing her state the very words I had just spoken served as a kind of shock to my system. I suddenly felt as if I were receiving a revelation from an angel on high, and I realized that her question pointed directly to an area in which I was in great error. I said to myself in awe, "She is right! All people's deaths are great deaths!" Then I scolded myself: "You are trying to sell Chinul's death to this audience at the expense of the death that is experienced by billions of people? How wrong you are!" The woman's words, I now saw, served to protect the great dignity of the deaths of all the ordinary people in the world. I felt severely chastened.

I also saw, however, that no matter how anyone dies, the entire experience itself lies within the realm of *momjit*. Thus, if someone, such as an enlightened Zen master, wishes to control or manipulate the time and circumstances of his death, he may certainly do so. Yet does this make his death more noble than that of someone who lacks such a capability? I believe that the most important aspect of death is that it heralds our return back to *mom*. Some people are fortunate enough to reach this valuable understanding before their own death. They are aware that they will be returning back to the God who created them. Even more fortunate are those who are able to see that life and death are not opposing forces, the one good and the other bad. To investigate and come to an understanding of the true nature of death is extremely important, I believe, if we are to lead a meaningful, conflict-free life. In my understanding, death represents a complete negation of everything we have ever known. In this sense, it can be called an achievement of the First Revolution, as discussed earlier. This experience of negation is available to all of us, however, even before we die physically. We can die many times within the course of a lifetime or even within a single day; what is required, though, is nothing less than the complete abandonment of all our previously held notions. Painful as this may be, it is only at this point that we may discover some insight into our own lives and into the nature of life as a whole. This, then, is what is referred to as the "great death." Its most fundamental nature is that of forgiveness, for at this time the slate is wiped clean, so to speak. It is most important to understand, however, that this "great death" is something that can only be reached through experience; it is useless to speculate about it from our ordinary, limited, *momjit* perspective.

Despite the inestimable value of such an experience, however, I maintain that all deaths are "great deaths." Death is not only a complete negation, but a complete affirmation as well. Although it may of necessity be described differently according to the cultural origin of the person describing it, it is universally experienced as a moment of enlightenment, or *nirvāṇa*. If one can investigate the nature of death while he is still young, strong, and successful, then he may be fortunate enough to understand how truly great death is. It is the end of *momjit*, but not of *mom*. It is a time of glory, a time for celebration; we are returning to the *mom*.

I would like to close with a short comment on the death of Jesus Christ. It is believed that his last words, as he hung from the cross, were, "My God, why have you forsaken me?" These are obviously words that express the most profound grief and disillusion. Many people find it painful to be reminded of these despairing words. Yet I believe that if he had held a different attitude, for example a feeling of happiness that he was returning to his Father, the entire history of Christianity would have proceeded much differently. If Jesus had died with a smile on his face, glad to be leaving this world of suffering, what would the people have thought? They may have wished that they, too, could leave the world and join their Creator in heaven. Thus, they would be seeking an escape from reality, an empty illusion. Jesus' death on the cross, then, ultimately represents the achievement of a complete negation. We, too, need to do this, for how can we help others unless we give up our own selves?

CHAPTER THREE

Other Teachings

One of the fascinating things about the *mom/momjit* paradigm is that it may be used to help us discover a deeper dimension to other religious teachings. In this chapter, I would like to investigate a few of these other schools of thought as well as some of the various Buddhist teachings and scriptures, and discuss how the nondualistic truth of *mom/momjit* may be applied to them.

WŎNHYO'S *COMMENTARY ON THE AWAKENING OF MAHĀYĀNA FAITH* (FIRST CHAPTER)

Many people, when learning about the terms *mom* and *momjit* for the first time, mistakenly believe that they are identical to the well-known paradigm of *t'i* and *yung*, which originated in China. I say "mistakenly," because although the *mom/momjit* model has certain similarities to that of *t'i/yung*, it is by no means identical to it. Briefly stated, *t'i* refers to the inner, invisible dimension of existence, whereas *yung* represents the outer, visible aspect. I do not wish to expand on the meaning and significance of these terms, as I have already done so in my previous book, *Buddhist Faith and Sudden Enlightenment*. I would like to say here, though, that the concepts of *t'i* and *yung* have a very lengthy historical background, and to comprehend them correctly requires that one have an understanding of various other related systems of thought, such as the German debate concerning substance and phenomena, as well as the fundamental principles of Aristotelian thought. In my opinion, the comprehension of *mom* and *momjit* is a much less burdensome task. Their meaning may be much more easily grasped, in the sense that each one of us possesses a body (*mom*) and uses that body on a daily basis (*momjit*). This has already been discussed earlier. When we begin to read Wŏnhyo's works we may discover, to our relief, that he sympathizes with the need to educate people at a level which they can most easily comprehend. With regard to his commentary on Asvaghoṣa's treatise, *The Awakening of Mahāyāna Faith*, the first chapter of which we will examine here, it is evident that he does not wish for his readers to merely accumulate more knowledge, but rather is intent on their grasping the essential message of the treatise.

Who was Wŏnhyo? A Korean monk of the seventh century, he is considered Korea's most prolific writer on Buddhism. It is believed that he authored more than 250 texts, of which only about twenty-three are extant. His *Commentary on The Awakening of Mahāyāna Faith*, discussed here, is deemed by scholars to be the most popular and influential of all the commentaries associated with this text. His message, which is clearly one of nondualism, is succinctly covered in the first chapter of his commentary, entitled "On Revealing the Essence of The Doctrine." Although it consists of only five short paragraphs, this chapter aptly imparts a comprehensive view of Wŏnhyo's insightful understanding. In the first paragraph he says he does not know what to call the "essence," which exists everywhere. He notes that others have called it "completely empty" or "very mysterious," yet he evidently feels that these terms do not adequately describe its true nature. We may observe that in this paragraph he makes no attempt to define this essence in terms of *mom* or *momjit*, as he realizes that there is no way in which he can do so. His primary concern here is the essence itself, and not the meanings of *mom* and *momjit*, or their relationship with each other. It is virtually impossible to manifest the meaning of these two terms linguistically, let alone to define the essence of Mahāyāna. As soon as you attach a label to it, says Wŏnhyo, then immediately its opposing characteristics emerge. For example, he states:

> . . . No matter how mysterious it may be,
> How could it be anywhere but in the
> world of myriad phenomena?
> No matter how empty it may be,
> it is still present in the conversation of the people.[1]

Clearly, words such as "empty" or "mysterious" do not suffice. What else is to be done, then, except to abandon all attempts at definition whatsoever? This is the conclusion Wŏnhyo arrives at, and he at last admits, "I do not know how to describe it; therefore, I am compelled to call it the Great Vehicle."[2] He ends this paragraph with a question: "Who can awaken deep faith in the state of no-thought?"[3] This "state of no-thought" is evidently a reference to Wŏnhyo's term "Great Vehicle," that essence which may be alluded to but never properly defined. We may pose further questions: Does this state exist in human beings? May we gain access to it?

In the second paragraph of this chapter, Wŏnhyo praises Asvaghoṣa's great compassion and wisdom. He does this using experiential terms rather than viewing these qualities in an intellectual or cognitive sense. Asvaghoṣa's compassion is described as follows: "[H]e was distressed over those people whose minds, moved by the winds of ignorance and delusion, are easily tossed about," and, "[H]e was grieved that the true nature of Original Enlightenment . . . is difficult to awaken."[4] Furthermore, with regard to Asvaghoṣa's great wisdom, Wŏnhyo stated that he possessed "the power of wisdom by which one regards others as his own body . . ."[5]

This entire paragraph has a positive, affirmative tone and is very uplifting for the reader, in contrast to the thorough attack on all languages and concepts, which leads us to a bleak sense of utter negation, in the preceding paragraph. Indeed, these two paragraphs form an effective balance, the affirmation of the latter neatly offsetting the negation of the former. We might say that in order for Asvaghoṣa's great wisdom and compassion to be demonstrated, Wŏnhyo needed first to outline the fundamental issue, that is, the complete impossibility of defining the essence of existence in linguistic terms. Why is this? Is it perhaps because the praiseworthy qualities of wisdom and compassion can only be derived from one's ability to first arrive at an understanding of the negative nature of reality? Truly, this existence of ours cannot be correctly comprehended through the use of our limited sense faculties. With this awareness comes the desire to help others, not only to enable them to see the same truth on an intellectual level, but to also awaken them on the experiential plane. As Wŏnhyo states, with reference to Asvaghoṣa:

> He wished to cause scholars . . . to completely extract the meaning of Tripiṭaka; he wished to cause practitioners to permanently stop myriad illusory phenomena and finally return to the source of One Mind.[6]

The third paragraph is a relatively minor one in comparison with the previous two. Wŏnhyo discusses Asvaghoṣa's treatise as successfully synthesizing all the various aspects of Buddhist truth, as expounded in its many scriptures. Thus, he states: "By revealing two aspects in One Mind, it comprehensively includes the one hundred and eight jewels of the Mahāyāna teaching."[7] Here, he uses the phrase "two aspects in One Mind" as a doctrinal device to assert the effectiveness and all-inclusive nature of Asvaghoṣa's treatise. Unfortunately, people are too often unaware of these two aspects, the relative and the absolute, operating within them. Although many of us understand the importance of One Mind, at least on an intellectual level, our day-to-day thoughts and behavior are generally not consciously conducted from this understanding. We experience many contradictions and conflicts due to the existence of the relative aspect. The absolute and relative aspects are often experienced as a discrepancy, and this causes us much confusion and pain. Wŏnhyo felt that Asvaghoṣa was able to successfully point to this problem by creating the phrase "two aspects in One Mind." He felt that this phrase penetrated to the core of the issue and that with it all the 84,000 scriptures of Buddhism could be successfully understood. Furthermore, Wŏnhyo felt that this treatise was the only one that successfully penetrates the essence of all the scriptures, as it "comprehensively embrac[es] the limitless" teachings of Buddhism.

Paragraph four, although crucial in terms of understanding Wŏnhyo's message, is at the same time often misunderstood and indeed has been the subject of much controversy among scholars. In this paragraph Wŏnhyo investigates the message of the treatise on a deeper level, through the use of the terms *unfolding* and *sealing* (or "folding"). As I consider this paragraph the focal one of the chapter, I will quote it in its entirety:

> Such being the intent of this treatise, when unfolded, there are immeasurable and limitless meanings to be found in its doctrine; when sealed, the principle of two aspects in One Mind is found to be its essence. Within the two aspects are included myriad meanings without confusion. These limitless meanings are identical with One Mind and are completely amalgamated with it. Therefore, it unfolds and seals freely; it establishes and refutes without restrictions. Unfolding but not complicating; sealing but not narrowing; establishing but gaining nothing; refuting but losing nothing—this is Asvaghoṣa's wonderful skill and the essence of the Awakening of Faith.[8]

This entire paragraph is an exemplary depiction of One Mind, which we have been calling *mom*. What is unfolded? And what is sealed? It is the principle of the two aspects in One Mind that is being thus described. Yet we must be careful not to perceive this as a kind of magical or mystical event. Rather, it occurs naturally and spontaneously all the time throughout the myriad activities of our everyday world. Here, in contrast to its philosophical implications as discussed in the previous paragraph, the phrase "two aspects in One Mind" is imparted with a more spiritual significance. Through the act of unfolding, Wŏnhyo says, the 84,000 doctrines, representing "immeasurable and limitless meanings," are explained, whereas through sealing all these doctrines are recognized as reflecting the essence of One Mind, or *mom*. In unfolding, then, all the various manifestations of *mom* appear in our lives; it is the scholar's task to investigate these manifestations. Sealing, on the other hand, refers to an atmosphere or state in which all phenomena have disappeared, for they have returned back to their source, *mom*. This state does not pertain to the philosophical or speculative arena but rather occurs solely through spiritual practice, the practice of meditation. Wŏnhyo's special ability was his insistence on placing primary importance on the seeker's task, that is, on the practice and experience of meditation itself. To be able to grasp this fundamental position assumed by Wŏnhyo is crucial for any serious reader of his works. In discussing concepts or various systems of thought, his attitude is consistently one of negation, as he realizes the impossibility of accurately depicting truth in affirmative terms. And whenever he does approach the positive dimension, he never fails to view it in terms of the unique principle of One Mind, the essence. Wŏnhyo is a scholar, yet the purpose of his scholarship is to raise people up to the level of practice. Similarly, throughout the Buddha's many, many years of teaching, he chose not to merely educate people on an intellectual or philosophical level, but rather to lead them to the same state he himself was experiencing. An identical understanding may be applied to the life and teachings of Jesus Christ.

This first chapter closes with a very short paragraph which imparts no new truths but is rather a type of lament with regard to the inability of people to correctly comprehend his message. Wŏnhyo concludes with a determination to continue correlating sections of the treatise with various Buddhist scriptures in the hopes that his readers may glean some new insights into the matter at hand.

WŎNHYO'S *TREATISE ON THE VAJRASAMĀDHI SŪTRA* (FIRST CHAPTER)

In the seventh century CE, Wŏnhyo wrote a treatise on the Vajrasamādhi Sūtra, a Buddhist pseudo-text that originated in China some two hundred years earlier. It is known as a pseudo-text because although it carries the title "sūtra," it does not present the words or writings of the Buddha himself. This sūtra is highly regarded, however, especially by Chinese Zen Buddhists.

The Sanskrit word *vajra* may be translated as "diamond." Why is this word used in reference to samādhi here? The essence of a diamond is its hardness, and its ability to resist any impact that strikes against it. In this sense, we may say that it is impenetrable. Similarly, in our attempts to achieve samādhi, we must resemble a diamond: we must be firm and unyielding. Our effort must stem from an iron will, yet we must at the same time realize that these efforts, although situated within the realm of *momjit*, are nevertheless an integral part of the world of *mom*, and are never for an instant isolated from it. Only with such an understanding will our practice ripen and bear fruit. If our perspective is tainted, however, by the three poisons of greed, anger, or ignorance, then it will lose its diamond-like quality and we will begin to backslide.

Although other scholars have commented on this sūtra, Wŏnhyo was the first to do so. His treatise provides substantial evidence to support my theory concerning the first and second revolutions in the spiritual life of a practitioner, as discussed earlier. Even though he does not specifically use the words *mom* and *momjit*, in the first section of his treatise, entitled "Presenting the Main Points of the Vajrasamādhi Sūtra," Wŏnhyo makes explicit use of this paradigm as a means of delineating his philosophical religious system of thought. I would now like to examine this section of Wŏnhyo's treatise in detail so that we may observe his deep understanding of the workings of the *mom/momjit* paradigm.

His first phrase states, "The source of one mind, departing both being and non-being, alone pure."[9] The key term here is "source of one mind." In my opinion, this phrase is not meant to imply that one mind has a separate source that exists apart from it, but rather that one mind is the source itself. A paraphrase of this would be: "the source which is one mind." This source, or one mind, is nothing other than *mom* in its universal aspect. With this phrase, "source of one mind," Wŏnhyo is skillfully making use of a pedagogical device called *upamā/upameya*, which was often used by traditional Buddhist writers to convey a more comprehensive meaning of an intended message. This Sanskrit word *upamā* means "simile," whereas *upameya* may be variously translated as "dharma," "message," "teaching," or "truth." The words which signify the *upamā/upameya* device always occur in apposition, as the first is used as a necessary reference point, or indicator, of the second. An example of such a device from East Asian

Buddhist literature is "the finger which points to the moon." In this phrase the *upamā* is the finger, which refers directly to the *upameya*, the moon. The message or truth here is the moon, which in Buddhist jargon represents the state or experience of enlightenment. The simile of the finger, then, is used to indicate any device or method which brings one into direct contact with that state or experience.

In Wŏnhyo's phrase, "the source of one mind," the word *source* is the simile which points to the message of "one mind." Without the presence of this simile of the "source," we might not understand precisely what "one mind" is. However, with the mere addition of this one word, "source," we are led to the awareness that "one mind" is the origin from which all else arises. Again, the meaning here is "the source which is one mind."

In the next part of the phrase, "departing both being and non-being," Wŏnhyo is indicating the nondualistic nature of one mind. It is concerned neither with what exists nor with what does not exist, but rather "departs" from, or transcends, both meanings. Thus, a state of complete "isness" or "suchness" is depicted. This state lies far apart from the phenomenal word of *momjit*; such is the quality of universal *mom*. The term "alone pure" indicates that this one mind is unequalled in the sense of being utterly undefiled and unapproachable.

This first phrase, then, clearly refers to *mom* as it exists in its universal aspect, in which it stands apart from all being and all non-being. Wŏnhyo's next statement, however, has an entirely different cast to it. He writes: "The sea of triple emptiness, interpenetrating both the sacred and the profane, so transparent."[10] The nature of *mom* changes here; it now becomes involved in the world of phenomena. This is *mom* in its individual aspect, which appears to unenlightened people as *momjit*, performing the action or function of infusing itself into the substance of all phenomena, both sacred and profane. We are permitted here to see the enlightened prospective, in which *momjit* is understood to be not separate from but rather an aspect of *mom*, the aspect of function or usage. The sea of triple emptiness is itself *mom*, but through its action of absorbing itself into the sacred and profane, it (and thus they themselves, that is, all phenomena), appears to the world as *momjit*.

We might note that Wŏnhyo again uses the *upamā/upameya* device in the phrase "sea of triple emptiness." Here, the word *sea* is used as a simile to refer to the message of "emptiness." References to water or the ocean are often used by Buddhist writers who wish to convey the idea of a source point. Here Wŏnhyo uses the word *sea* to imply a similar meaning, that of an origin or departure point from which everything flows outward into the universe. We have previously discussed the fact that for Buddhists the ultimate source is emptiness, and this is undoubtedly why Wŏnhyo chose to describe the sea in such a way. Emptiness is indeed a reflection of the universal *mom*. We must remember, too, that in Buddhist doctrine this state or experience of emptiness is not meant to indicate a state of nothingness, but rather just the opposite: it is a fullness, an openness or transparency, in which everything in the universe is reflected. It is a state of ultimate receptivity, and is referred to here as "triple" because it may refer to any or all of three realities: there may be emptiness of self, emptiness of an object, or emptiness of emptiness itself.

I would like to point out here my choice of the word *interpenetrating* for the Chinese term *wu-ai*. Other translators have used terms such as "dissolving" or "amalgamating," yet these words give the impression that through their action the sacred and profane suffer a loss of boundaries and thus identity. However, it is clear that this is not Wŏnhyo's intention, as we may see in the following phrase, which states "yet not one." Thus, although both the sacred and profane are charged with a special significance due to the presence of *mom* (the sea of triple emptiness) within them, this does not mean that they somehow "dissolve" or "amalgamate" into a mystical union. The sacred still remains sacred and the profane remains profane. It is through the interpenetration, or infusion, of *mom* that their identities are seen as transformed, yet they remain unquestionably as they are.

Similarly, of crucial importance is the word *transparent* for the Chinese term *yüan-rung*. This character may also be translated as "clear" or "placid," yet I prefer the term *transparent* as it aids the reader in understanding the fact that through the interpenetration by *mom*, the two phenomenal realms, sacred and profane, are rendered utterly open and available to all the myriad influences and manifestations of the universe. They become imbued with *mom's* essential quality of emptiness so that they, too, possess it. In the sense, then, that all phenomena share this quality of emptiness, they are said to be not separated from *mom*, or emptiness, itself.

Wŏnhyo's third phrase, "So transparent, interpenetrating the two, yet not one,"[11] is a recapitulation of the preceding phrase, making clear the understanding, as explained above, that each of the two realms of sacred and profane maintains its own identity. Each, though interpenetrated by *mom*, remains as it is; the two are two, "not one."

The fourth phrase reads, "Alone pure, departing the extremes, yet not the middle way."[12] Here Wŏnhyo returns to a discussion of universal *mom*, with the additional information that although it does not abide with the extreme position, it does not rest at the middle way either. Now, our casual understanding of the middle is that it is situated between two opposites or extremes. In early Buddhism, however, this term "the middle way" had a special connotation; it referred to the Buddha's state of enlightenment. Prior to his awakening, before he left home to begin his spiritual quest, his life was spent fully absorbed in material concerns; indeed, he was surrounded by conditions of unsurpassed wealth. Certainly he must have initially been very content with and undoubtedly attached to such a lifestyle. Then, after encountering a sick person, an old person, a corpse, and finally a monk, he began to question his life and see it as unsatisfactory. Eventually, he could no longer tolerate his own inner sense of suffering and he felt compelled to leave home and begin his wandering in search of freedom. However, as he began to perform various spiritual disciplines in quest of his goal, he gradually became attached to the other extreme, the sacred or spiritual. He lived in this way for six years, having moved from a position of attachment to materiality to that of attachment to spirituality. Finally, upon becoming enlightened he realized that these two states were not opposites as he had previously assumed, but rather represented two aspects of one unity, which he called emptiness. This understanding, which utterly negates the typical "either-or" construction of reality, might be perceived as a kind of relativism; in Buddhism, it is called "the middle way," and to understand it experientially signifies a state of enlightenment or awakening. Therefore, when Wŏnhyo says that one mind, while departing from the extremes, does not represent the middle way either, he is making a very radical statement. What he is really saying is this: Don't take the Buddha's way. Don't follow the middle, even if it is considered the enlightened way, for if you do, you are merely creating another dualistic pair of opposites, that of the extremes on one side and enlightenment on the other. Thus, in Wŏnhyo's mind, to posit the middle way, or enlightenment, as being of greater value than the two extremes is to assume a dangerously dualistic stance. Wishing to avoid such a position, he simply says, "not the middle way."

In phrase five Wŏnhyo states, "not the middle way, yet departing the extremes. So dharma of no being does not occupy non-being. Phenomena of no non-being do not occupy being."[13] At this point Wŏnhyo has completed his definitions of *mom* and *momjit*, with which he was preoccupied in the preceding four phrases, and proceeds with a description of what occurs at the First Revolution. As we have discussed earlier, in this revolution, also called Stage One, the practitioner undergoes an experience of complete negation. All language, all concepts, are denied or eliminated and thus negated as a means of severing our attachment to them. Whatever understanding we may have, even of *mom* or enlightenment itself, must of necessity be attacked at this stage, for the understanding we hold in our present state of consciousness can never be the correct one, in an ultimate or absolute sense. Here, in his usual way, Wŏnhyo first repeats the message of the previous phrase ("not the middle way, yet departing the extremes"), and then goes on to impart a new message. Basically, the gist of his new message is: Not-A is not not–A and No not-A is not A either. These statements are referred to in Buddhist doctrines as "double negation." I call them "complete negation," as they represent the utter denial of any affirmative aspect of existence (or nonexistence) whatsoever. More simply, we might say: Being is not being, or John is not John. The implication here is that since each phenomenon of the universe, including John or any being we may apprehend (and this applies to concepts as well), is inherently empty, and thus "transparent," it or he is inescapably open to the influence of all other phenomena. Thus, he (or it) will undoubtedly contain a myriad number of aspects or identities within himself (in addition, of course, to being John). John, then, is not merely John; how can he be when he contains the essences of so many others? We may remember the metaphor of Indra's net; there, each pearl is not an isolated entity unto itself but rather a mirror in which all the other pearls are reflected, just as it is reflected in all the other pearls, which themselves are mirrors as well.

Just as phrase five refers to *mom* through its reference to being, or essence, phrase six reflects the realm of *momjit* through its statements concerning action. Wŏnhyo states, "Not one, yet interpenetrating the two, so phenomena not sacred have not acted profane. Principle not profane has not acted sacred."[14] This is another example of a double, or complete, negation and serves a similar purpose to the previous phrase. The negation this time, however, is one of action or manifestation.

The successful completion of this stage may be said to indicate a state of enlightenment on the part of the practitioner. A problem may easily arise at this point, however, if one becomes attached to this state of negation. Such an attachment might easily lead one to become a victim of nihilism. This is why the Second Revolution, as indicated by the last two phrases, seven and eight, is necessary. In phrase seven Wŏnhyo states, "Dissolving the two, yet not one. So natures both sacred and profane nowhere do not stand. Phenomena both tainted and pure never do not manifest."[15] Here, then, is established a complete affirmation of all phenomena, both sacred and profane, tainted and pure. They exist everywhere with no obstructions. Phrase eight is an affirmation of a similar nature, only now all doctrines and dharmas, both of being and non-being, so and not-so, are affirmed: "Departing the extremes, yet not the middle way. So dharmas of both being and non-being nowhere do not work. Doctrines of both so and not-so never do not apply."[16] We should be careful to understand here, however, that this level of practice does not represent final enlightenment, as one can still be attached to his intellectual understanding.

WŎNHYO'S LOGIC OF NEGATION

I would now like to focus on one particular passage in Wŏnhyo's treatise which is located in the section entitled "Narration of its Principal Ideas." In this section Wŏnhyo discusses what he calls the "fountainhead of the one mind" in various ways. At one point he makes the following statement:

> ... while nothing is negated, there is nothing not negated;
> while nothing is established, there is nothing not established.
> This can be called the ultimate principle ...[17]

Many translations of this passage from the original classical Chinese have appeared, especially in Korea, as the contributions of Wŏnhyo to the field of Korean Buddhism have gained increasing attention. Yet none of the translations that I have seen differ to any significant degree from that which I have just cited. Furthermore, and most important for my argument here, they are all written from a decidedly Taoist, as opposed to a Buddhist, perspective. As Wŏnhyo himself was a noted Buddhist, and not a Taoist, thinker, I thus feel that these translations do not do adequate justice to his intended message

What is my basis for making such a claim? One of the most fundamental tenets of Taoist thought is the principle of *wu-wei*, which may be translated as "no action" or "non-activity." This concept may be seen as a metaphor for nature itself (Chinese: *tzu-ran*). We should note here that the Eastern understanding of nature differs quite radically from that of the Western world. In the West, nature is viewed as an objective realm; man is free to enjoy it or destroy it according to his will, for it is seen to exist purely as an object, outside himself. For Easterners, however, nature encompasses everything, including man, for it is *mom* itself. Lao-tzu, considered by many to be the "father" of Taoism, was constantly drawing people's attention to nature. His message was essentially that it does nothing, yet there is nothing it does not do. This is also the meaning of *wu-wei*. It is not meant to reflect a state of immobility, in which no movement whatsoever occurs, but rather points to a "doing without doing."

When Buddhist practitioners arrived in China from India, they made use of this term *wu-wei* as a means of helping the Chinese people to better understand the meaning of the Buddhist term *enlightenment*. In our contemporary world, the concept of *wu-wei* has been adopted unquestioningly by many Buddhists who feel that it is an essential aspect of Buddhist thought. Yet in doing so, they are remaining in ignorance of the intention of the Buddha's teachings, which was to point to the truth of human suffering and how it may be eliminated. I will elaborate on this in just a minute, but for now, let us return to the passage which I previously cited and investigate its meaning. When Wŏnhyo writes, "nothing is negated" what is he saying? The words used here reflect a state in which no action of negation exists. Similarly, the words "nothing is established" suggest that no affirmation is present either. According to the Chinese word used, *li*, "established" here has the same meaning as "affirmed." The message as it appears here, then, is twofold: nothing is denied yet nothing is affirmed. This interpretation, as I stated above, corresponds quite closely with the Taoist view of nature; it is an ontological perspective, denoting the quality of nature itself. I am critical of this interpretation, as I feel that the Buddha's message was a different one. I also believe that Wŏnhyo himself, a committed follower of Buddhist teachings, never intended to convey the Taoist message of *wu-wei*. Let us now examine this issue further.

First of all, it is my belief that the Buddha's teaching cannot be accurately understood without an acknowledgment of the deep significance of his radical act of leaving home. This act represented an expression of his desire for wisdom, or a higher level of consciousness, and thus we may say that it reflected an upward spiritual direction. Subsequently, after he attained enlightenment, his direction moved downward; he returned back to the secular world and spread his message to others. Without the initial thrust, represented by his act of leaving home, he would not have been able to begin his upward quest. We might note here that it may be entirely possible to "leave home" without ever crossing your doorstep. What is of crucial importance is what the act of leaving home implies, which is moving away, either literally or symbolically, from one's old, familiar, cherished perceptions about himself and his life. For the Buddha, this moving away from the familiar was a radical physical experience in which he left both home and family, wandering from place to place for six years while studying with a number of teachers, seeking answers to his questions concerning the truth of existence. In this way he was learning to negate, step by step, all of his previous conceptions about himself and his life. Later, he was able to assert the value of what he had learned from this negation process, but the initial experience of complete negation, which was a type of renunciation, was essential.

Now let us return to the passage in the treatise that we have been discussing. As I said before, I do not feel that the words "nothing is negated" accurately reflect the Buddha's experience. These words, stated thus, represent an affirmation, for if nothing is negated then everything is affirmed. Yet the Buddha's experience, as we have seen, and his initial teaching as well, begin in just the opposite direction: they are a negation. In addition, we need to note that for any teaching to be labeled Buddhist, it must begin with the human element, with man's unavoidable condition of suffering, his basic sense of dissatisfaction with life. It does not begin, as Taoist teachings do, with an ontological statement about the nature of reality in which "nothing is negated." Rather, the first of the Buddha's discourses to his disciples following his enlightenment experience delineates what are called the Four Noble Truths, and the first of these truths states that life, all life, is inevitably accompanied by the experience of suffering. This in itself may be seen as a type of negation, as it reflects a negative perspective of life. This understanding of our own dissatisfaction is crucial if we are ever to attain awakening, for how can we arrive at the affirmative experience of enlightenment unless we first realize its inherent negative aspect?

Now I would like to briefly discuss my reasons for feeling that Wŏnhyo himself would not have approved of the Taoist interpretation of this passage, which is in such widespread existence today. We have previously investigated his first chapter entitled "Presenting the Main Points," in which he outlines his summary of the Vajrasamādhi Sūtra. In this chapter, he clearly depicts the nature of one mind and its corresponding "sea of triple emptiness": describing them first as a negation, which I have termed the First Revolution, and then as an affirmation, or Second Revolution. Clearly, then, Wŏnhyo sees the importance of a sequential process from the negative to the positive. Indeed, he supports this position by immediately following this particular discussion with the word *hence*. In this way, I feel, he is putting his stamp of approval on my argument here, thus corroborating my assertion concerning his intent.

At this point I would like to offer what I feel is a more accurate interpretation of the passage, one that more closely reflects Wŏnhyo's intended message. The classical Chinese words for this phrase are: *wu po erh wu pu po*. It is the word *wu* here that is in question; its traditional translation has been rendered as "nothing." However, I see this first *wu* as representing a strong, dynamic action, the act of negation itself. Thus, instead of reading "nothing is negated," I believe the passage should read, "negation is negated." In my opinion, it is a mistake to interpret this phrase as meaning that no negation occurs. Rather, *wu* is aggressive and we are led to realize that all negation is negated. If we read the phrase in this way, there can be no mistake concerning its negative meaning. Not able to be turned into an affirmation, it remains an utter negation. Similarly, in the first part of the second phrase, which has been traditionally translated as "nothing is established," I would like to change it to "establishment is negated." Here again, as a result of this change, the meaning of the phrase is altered to represent a negation, whereas its original translation reflects just the opposite, an affirmation. Thus, my altered translation of the entire passage reads as follows:

> While negation is negated,
>   there is nothing not negated.
> While establishment (affirmation) is negated,
>   there is nothing not established.

As you can see, I have not altered the second half of either sentence. I see no need to change these phrases, as they aptly reflect the condition represented by the Second Revolution, in which establishment, or affirmation, is now permitted and endorsed. With the changes I have installed in the first half of each sentence, however, the sequence from negation to affirmation has been correctly delineated. With this new translation, I feel confident that the Buddha's teachings have been accurately conveyed.

HUA-YEN THEORY

I would now like to briefly discuss the teachings of the Hua-yen sect of Buddhism as they relate to the *mom/momjit* paradigm. This sect, which originated in China in the seventh century and is still widely practiced in the Far East today, espouses a four-stage process of understanding or awakening. I will briefly delineate these stages, which may also be termed levels or dharma (truth) realms.

The first stage may be called the dharma realm of affairs or events (Chinese: *shih*). This stage is entirely concerned with the world of phenomena, whether visible or invisible. Thus, phenomena here include not only all physical objects, but mental, emotional, and bodily processes as well. Anything that can be expressed or described may thus be termed *shih*. This, of course, is what I have been calling *momjit*. It may further be stated that every *shih* has its own self-nature or identity, which is exclusive of every other identity. For example, paper is paper; it is not water. This stage exists at the most primal level of awareness; here, one's consciousness is very shallow and he is concerned primarily with his own profit, his own security. Each human being is seen as an individual, independent entity, who is in constant competition with others for his own survival. This is the shortcoming of the capitalistic way of life. There is no perception of a larger dimension to existence. All living beings are viewed as being imprisoned within their five (or six, if you include the mind) senses: "What you see is what you get." Life is viewed as a constant struggle.

The second stage is called the dharma realm of principle (Chinese: *li*). Here, everything in the universe may be seen in terms of this one unifying principle, as it penetrates all phenomena. Many people view *li* as *mom* itself. In Buddhism it is called the Buddha-nature, whereas Judeo-Christian adherents label it God, who is believed to be the Creator of all the myriad phenomena of the universe. This quality of *li* may refer to human-originated principles as well, such as the principle of relativity as discovered by Einstein, the principle of gravity as first observed by Isaac Newton, the economic principle as espoused by Karl Marx, and so forth. The problem with this realm is that anyone abiding here will inevitably experience a conflict, or sense of differentiation and separation, between *shih* and *li*, or phenomenon and principle. People who remain at this level have yet to resolve the issue of the relationship between the two qualities. As a result, those abiding within this realm are often contemptuous of those in the first realm, feeling superior due to their belief that they have discovered God, whose presence those in the first realm remain ignorant of. Yet although their awareness of principle is laudable, they may easily become attached to this same principle and thus create a painful gap between themselves and those abiding in the lower realm of *shih*.

The third realm, which is the dharma realm of no obstruction between *shih* and *li*, successfully resolves the above difficulty. It is called *li shih wu ai*, and literally translates as "no obstruction or hindrance between *shih* and *li*." Those at this level of understanding are aware that *li*, or principle, far from being apart or separate from *shih*, actually abides within all *shih*, within all phenomena. In this realm, nothing can be denigrated or denied in any way, for the complete harmonization of opposites has been achieved. Spinoza's philosophy of pantheism may be seen to exist quite comfortably here, as well as the theories of the two Chung brothers of twentieth-century China. The latter gained extensive recognition for their assertion that *li*, symbolizing the One, exists within all *shih*, the many. *Li* can thus be seen to exist within such disastrous circumstances as the war in Iraq, the aftermath of hurricane Katrina, the collapse of Wall Street, and a person dying of terminal cancer. This understanding helps to prevent and/or dissolve the arising of discrimination against others, and fosters compassion and the desire to alleviate suffering. As *li* does not exist apart from *shih*, the Buddha exists even within an ignorant sentient being. Because of this all-pervading presence of *li*, then, all *shih* may be seen as protected and cared for. The problem here, however, is that *li* is still viewed as occupying a higher position than *shih*, for without the initial awareness of *li*, *shih* cannot be adequately understood. Thus, harmonization can only be accomplished through the presence of *li*, as *shih* is not able to stand alone, unsupported. Because of this, *li* tends to become a crutch to be depended upon, and its importance can easily become exaggerated out of all proportion. One's understanding may then become distorted or biased, as in the case of fundamentalists or fanatics who ascribe all sorts of contrived characteristics to their view of *li*, or in this case, God.

For this reason the fourth dharma realm, *shih shih wu ai*, was devised. *Shih shih wu ai* translates as "no obstruction between one event and another." Here, the recognition of *li* disappears, and only *shih* remains. However, this is not the same *shih* that we encountered at the first level, for this *shih* is understood to contain *li* within it. Here, however, as opposed to the third level, the importance of *li* is not belabored or emphasized. It must be understood, however, that it is due to the fact of *li's* vast all-pervasiveness that it is not verbalized or described as such. Although *shih* may be said to embody *li*, *li* does not need to be acknowledged in order for *shih* to manifest. It is tacitly understood that *shih* contains *li*. An analogy would be the existence of light. Light is always with us, yet we do not feel the need to constantly express our awareness of this fact. A well-known saying with regard to this fourth level is: "In a speck of dust [*shih*] the whole world [*li*] is included." In Buddhist terms, we can say that even a speck of dust contains the Buddha. Since this is so, there is no need to acknowledge the Buddha's presence—he is already there.

The world of *shih shih wu ai* is the world of enlightened beings and can only be experienced through personal transformation. Once one has undergone such a transformation, however, he need not emphasize or even attest to his enlightened state. This fourth stage is the highest level that one can achieve in the physical form, and may be referred to as a wishless state. For an ordinary sentient being who aspires to reach this level, making a vow or having a goal is necessary, as it serves as a tool to help him attain the higher level. For an enlightened Buddha, however, everything in existence is experienced as a unity, as one, so what is there to wish for? Since nothing exists apart from this unity, what is there to be acknowledged or emphasized?

With regard to *mom* and *momjit*, we may see that the first level relates to the world of *momjit*, in which one has no awareness of the existence of the *mom* within which *momjit* abides. People on this level live in a realm of thoughts, emotions, and actions—and little else. In the second realm they begin to be aware of *mom* as the source of these same thoughts, emotions, and actions. Yet in their enthusiasm regarding this discovery, they often create a distorted view of *mom*, in which they see it as something apart from their thoughts, feelings, and deeds. In the third stage, the perception of separation disappears, yet people still cannot avoid espousing a *mom* that embraces all *momjit*. Finally, in the fourth realm, the need to assert the existence of *mom* is eliminated; *mom* has now been seen as completely integrated within *momjit*. In the context of Christianity, people abiding in this realm do not *love* God so much as they see themselves, and everything in their lives, including all others, *as* God. Although many saints may be said to occupy the third realm, very few people—perhaps only such sages as the Buddha and Jesus Christ—have attained the level of unity symbolized by the fourth realm of *shih shih wu ai*. Similarly, although this fourth level may be found within all spiritual traditions, it is not often easy to locate. This does not mean that all religions do not acknowledge it, but rather that it is not the usual way of understanding as held by religious practitioners. The process of transformation leading to the highest state is available to all, but rare is the person who is willing to tread such a path and see it through to the end.

THE DIAMOND SŪTRA

The Buddhist teachings have been compiled over hundreds and thousands of years into countless numbers of scriptures—indeed, some scholars estimate their number to be around 84,000. For Korean Buddhists, the Diamond Sūtra is considered to be the most valuable of all the scriptures in terms of daily practice. This is mainly due to the fact that this sūtra is directly concerned with meditation, that is, the process of emptying one's mind. The core message of the Diamond Sūtra is intended to help free us from all mental restrictions, both internal and external. This is why it is classified as a "wisdom" text: it points to the wisdom generated by an empty mind.

Specifically, in section two of this highly regarded Mahāyāna Sūtra, the monk Subhuti questions the Buddha about how to control thoughts. After praising Subhuti for raising such an important issue, the Buddha offers his advice regarding the matter, stating that all seekers, or "Bodhisattva-Heroes," should vow to bring all living creatures, or sentient beings, to a state of "Unbounded Liberation Nirvāṇa." Thus, he is exhorting Subhuti, as well as all spiritual seekers, to make a strong determination to save, or liberate, the entire realm of sentient beings. We may find a similar passage in the final chapter of the Hua-yen Sūtra, which concludes with Samantabhadra's vow to accomplish that very same purpose. The importance of this initial act of making a vow cannot be overemphasized; it represents a crucial departure point for practice which is necessary for any serious spiritual seeker.

At this point, however, the Buddha makes what may seem to the uninitiated to be a very surprising and remarkable statement. He declares that the truth of the matter is that no matter how strong one's vow, in actuality no sentient beings are saved. This passage, which espouses the doctrine of *anātman*, or no-self, reflects the core of Buddhist thought. As the Buddha states:

> Yet when vast, uncountable, immeasurable numbers of beings have thus been liberated, verily no being has been liberated—Why is this, Subhuti? It is because no Bodhisattva who is a real Bodhisattva cherishes the idea of an ego-entity, a personality, a being or separated individuality.[18]

Thus, asks the Buddha, how can we hope to save all sentient beings if no such independent, individual entities exist? The vow, then, to save all sentient beings is impossible to achieve, for what is a sentient being? It is not merely one among many particularized egos, but rather embodies a nature that is vast, all-inclusive, and universal. According to the teachings of the Buddha, the entire realm of sentient beings may be found to exist within the confines of one sentient being. Thus, the meaning of salvation for a Buddhist is to realize all sentient beings as abiding within yourself. A true act of charity then, does not necessarily involve giving your leftovers to someone else, but rather requires the ability to see yourself as you really are. The important thing is not to perform some sacred act, but rather to make a vow to return to the realm of *mom*, in which all outer appearances (*momjit*) are merely reflections of the inner essence of *mom*. This is the way of authentic Buddhist practice, at least in the East Asian Buddhist tradition. With regard to the practice of charity, the Buddha, in section four, offers specific advice to Subhuti:

Furthermore, Subhuti, in the practice of charity
a Bodhisattva should be detached. That is to say,
he should practice charity without regard to appearances;
without regard to sound, odor, touch, flavor, or any quality.[19]

Such a practice is a *mom* practice; it is no longer my practice. To disregard the senses is to place them within the dimension of the universal *mom*, and to remove them from the confines of my personal *momjit* world. In this way, the Diamond Sūtra is showing us how to live in the present moment—right here, right now. We can see that its message is none other than the message of the *mom/momjit* paradigm. Furthermore, this message enables us to realize that we can create and develop a practice that is based on our vow to return to *mom*. We begin to see that this is indeed possible.

Yet again, such a practice is only possible if we have a clear understanding of *mom*, which in section five is labeled "The Ultimate Principle of Reality." In this section the Buddha declares:

Subhuti, wheresoever are material characteristics
there is delusion; but whoso perceives that all
characteristics are in fact no-characteristics,
perceives the Tathāgata (the Awakened One).[20]

This is a very clear statement of no-self and thus of nonduality. As we have discussed before, to attain such an awareness requires that we abandon all attachment to our ordinary ways of thinking. Although our body is continually and unceasingly functioning within an environment of nonduality, we are rarely, if ever, aware of this fact. Yet in our desire for spiritual realization, it is important that we not attempt to strive for a nondual state, but rather learn to recognize, over and over again, that it already exists within us, just as we are. This is probably more difficult for Westerners than for those raised in Asian countries, not because of any inherent differences between the two groups of individuals—for after all, people are basically the same wherever you go—but rather due to the immense differences between the two cultures themselves. Yet the truth expounded in the Diamond Sūtra is relevant to each and every one of us, regardless of the culture in which we have been raised.

THE SEMINAL MESSAGE OF THE PLATFORM SŪTRA

The Platform Sūtra has been greatly respected by Zen practitioners in East Asia; indeed, it is treated as if it were taught by the Buddha himself. That is why it is called a sūtra, even though it reflects the teachings of Hui-neng, the sixth patriarch of Zen, who lived in the seventh century AD, many centuries after the Buddha.

In the early twentieth century, a group of young Japanese scholars was sent to England to study textual criticism and methodology in the field of Biblical Christianity. After finishing their studies there, they returned to Japan, where they conducted extensive research. One of their accomplishments was a compilation of the entire set of Chinese Buddhist scriptures, which are called *taisho*. They were also extremely interested in the teachings put forth in the Platform Sūtra. At that time, the most popular translation of this well-known Zen text was called the Koshoji version. However, in the 1930s a group of English archeologists discovered a number of Buddhist texts in a cave called Tun-huang. One of these texts was the Platform Sūtra, and when it was examined carefully, it was seen to differ from the Koshoji version in several crucial ways. It was generally agreed that this newly discovered text, which was named the Tun-huang version, was an earlier rendition of the Koshoji version. It was believed to be written by one of Hui-neng's disciples, probably about one hundred years after the sixth patriarch's death. (The discovery of the Tun-huang version was mentioned in an earlier chapter of this book entitled "No-Thought.")

Actually, the prevailing theory is that the author of this Tun-huang version was a monk named Shen-hui, who founded the Northern school of Zen. Hui-neng was known as the founder of the Southern, or Sudden, school, and Shen-hui was Hui-neng's disciple. The following story about an encounter between these two practitioners has been handed down over the years. Once, when giving a sermon to his disciples, Hui-neng said, "I have one thing, which existed even before the creation of the world. It is with us now and will continue to exist after the world has ended. It is omnipresent, omnipotent, and cannot be described in any language." He then asked his audience, "What is this one thing?"

Thirteen-year-old Shen-hui stood up and said, "It is my Buddha-nature."

Hui-neng thereupon scolded him, saying, "If it is indeed your Buddha-nature, then Buddha's message will soon disappear. If you hold such an attitude, you will never be considered an authentic teacher. You will always be like the offspring of the second wife [a position of inferiority]."[21]

Shen-hui's answer reflects the teachings of the Northern school of Zen, which believes that enlightenment must proceed through gradual stages, thus positing a duality or opposition between the one striving for enlightenment and enlightenment itself. Hui-neng, of the Southern, or Sudden, school, maintained that no such dualism exists, and that enlightenment is inherently within each of us, at all times.

Although Hui-neng chastised Shen-hui for his answer, which conveyed a dualistic understanding (that is, there is something that exists called the Buddha-nature as opposed to nonexistence), modern Japanese scholars, using their newly acquired scientific approach, have discovered other areas of the Tun-huang text that clearly endorse Shen-hui's way of thinking. The consensus of these scholars is that the text has been tampered with and does not correctly reflect the ideas of its original author; thus, they feel it is not reliable.

Most traditional scholars have tended to accept these conclusions drawn by the modern scholars, offering little, if any, criticism of their scientific methods. Yet we need to be careful here and not endorse these methods too hastily. We need to examine in depth the claims that these modern scholars are making.

In my opinion, modern scholars are committing a grave error. Scholars in the field of religion need to understand that they are a breed apart from scholars in other fields. The field of religion itself should be distinguished as unique with regard to all other fields of study, as its aim is to investigate and acknowledge an awareness and understanding of oneness, of nonduality. The word *religion* is derived from the Latin *religare*, which means "to bind back together." All religious study, then, is a study of unity. Yet religious scholars neglect to understand this and instead treat their subject as if they were examining a specimen under a microscope. This indeed is the scientific method, but it should not be the only method by which religious scholars study their area of interest. The modern scientific methods, which include textural criticism, philology, historiography, and so forth, are worthwhile but only partially so. What is needed on the part of the scholar is the ability and willingness to go beyond the scientific method, so that he may begin to loosen his grip on his dualistic way of thinking. He needs to learn to embody the *wu* or "no" as advocated in the Platform Sūtra. If he is able to do this, then the *nien* or "thought" that ensues will not be the same *nien* or thought that existed previously. It will be a completely transformed thought, enabling the scholar to perceive his area of interest in a fundamentally different manner. His understanding will now be deeper, simpler, and more insightful than his earlier view. This new understanding will accord completely with the logic propagated by the Buddha, the logic that scholars by and large are ignoring.

Modern religious scholars need to be provided with further training than that offered by today's universities. They need to be trained in the logic of nondualism, which is reflected in the age-old East Asian paradigm of *t'i-yung* and of *mom/momjit*; this is also the logic of the Sudden Doctrine of Zen. In a theistic context, it is called the logic of God. This is not a human or scientific logic, but is one that is indispensable when studying the scriptural texts of any religion.

It is certainly valid to produce scientific evidence, as modern scholars are so well trained at doing. Yet the vital question to be asked is: Are they qualified to correctly interpret this evidence? Let us compare this modern method of analyzing scriptures with the system that was adhered to back in the days of the Tang dynasty in China. During that era, which was one of China's most culturally prosperous periods, many Indian Buddhist texts were being translated into classical Chinese. This involved a three-part process. First, each text that was to be translated was subjected to critical scrutiny by a carefully organized translation bureau. This bureau was funded by the emperor, and was often located within his palace. The text was translated from its original Sanskrit into classical Chinese by a linguistic specialist who possessed a thorough knowledge of both languages. The translation was then reviewed by Buddhist specialists who were familiar with Buddhist history and philosophy, so as to eliminate any errors made by the linguist. Finally, the text was examined by a seasoned practitioner, to ensure that it accorded with the principles of Buddhist practices. The text was then subjected to this three-part review *another two times* before being placed in the hands of an enlightened monk. If it met with his approval, it was given the status of *cheng-i* or "enlightened document."

Korea is now the only country in the world in which this in-depth practice still occurs. Here in the United States, we do not really know who is or is not qualified to proclaim a text *cheng-i*. Yet we should understand that when examining or discussing any spiritual scripture, a spiritual perspective is sorely needed. The translation of a text is not merely a mechanical or intellectual task. What is called for is a religious understanding, which reflects a nondualistic, nonseparatist view of the universe. This view lies beyond the realm of the human mind or intellect. Scholars need to realize the priceless value of developing and maintaining such a view.

CHINUL

Chinul and the Three Gates

The name of the Korean monk, Chinul (AD 1158–1210), who lived during the middle of the period known as the Koryo Dynasty, is a familiar one to most Koreans. Many Westerners are becoming acquainted with his name as well. His significance for Korean Buddhism lies in the fact that he made a strong effort to synthesize the two dominant trends of Buddhist thought that existed at his time. Buddhism was undergoing much turmoil during the Koryo Dynasty due to the seemingly antagonistic nature of these two trends. The one trend, influenced by Hua-yen teachings, favored an emphasis on an intellectual understanding of the Buddhist scriptures. The other trend, which derived from Zen, was purely meditative and was thus primarily concerned with one's own personal experience. Chinul sought to harmonize these two approaches; his understanding was as follows (I am paraphrasing him here):

> All Buddhist doctrines and scriptures come from the Buddha's mouth. Zen, however, came from the Buddha's mind. Yet as the Buddha's mouth and mind cannot be separated, neither should scriptural and Zen Buddhism be separated.[22]

This understanding earned Chinul recognition as the "great synthesizer" of the two streams of Buddhism in the Koryo Dynasty. Yet despite this title, many people do not have a clear picture of either the nature of his life or of the significance of his spiritual achievement. This is due in part to a rather one-sided, incomplete understanding of his writings as examined and discussed by various scholars, both Eastern and Western. As one primary example, if we read the inscription of the stele at Songgwang Monastery, where Chinul resided for eleven years, we find the following passage included within it:

> He opened up the three Gates (approaches to Son [Japanese: Zen] practice): first, the Gate of Balanced Maintenance of Alertness and Calmness, namely, the practical method of cultivation through simultaneous practice of meditation and wisdom; second, the Gate of Faith in and Understanding of the Perfect and Sudden Teaching, namely, the theoretical understanding of Son practice through the Hua-yen doctrine; and third, the Gate of the Direct Shortcut, namely, the paralogical technique of leading people directly to the experience of "awakening" through the *hwadu* . . .[23]

This passage is only a short part of a much longer text, which was written by a Confucian scholar named Kim Kunsu. Although the words are meant to impress us, if we read Chinul's own words we will find that the above statement does not accurately reflect either Chinul's own experience or his unique understanding of Buddhadharma (Buddhist truth). It is true that Chinul "opened up" the above-named three gates, but the complete picture is not quite as simple as stated above. What is not mentioned above is that by the end of his life, as a result of his thorough investigation of Buddhist principles, he arrived at an understanding that placed primary importance on the third gate, that of *hwadu* meditation, thus relegating the first two gates to a lesser position. It is certainly not the case that he created or devised three ways of understanding or practicing Buddhism, and then "opened" them up for the practitioner to choose from, as if the practitioner was in a department store, contemplating which merchandise to purchase. Rather, it was through his own lengthy and arduous struggle that Chinul finally, at the end of his life, arrived at a position of certainty regarding the superiority of the third gate, that of *hwadu* meditation. In an essay entitled "Resolving Doubts about Observing the *Hwadu*," he discussed his understanding at length. Regarding the other two gates, he criticized the dual practice of meditation and wisdom as lacking the acuity necessary for awakening, and claimed that the Hua-yen emphasis on faith and understanding was encumbered by its intellectual perspective, which prevented the seeker from reaching his/her goal of enlightenment. He firmly believed in the superior value of *hwadu* practice, as we are shown in the following passage: "Those of exceptional capacity in the Son school who investigate the *hwadu* closely and realize its subtlety do not give rise to the ten defects of knowledge and understanding."[24] He closes this text with the following: "I humbly hope that those who are intent on transcending the world through meditation will carefully investigate the live word of the Son approach [i.e., the *hwadu*] and swiftly realize *bodhi* [wisdom]."[25] We are clearly shown Chinul's enthusiastic endorsement of *hwadu* practice, and his belief that it is a superlative tool for awakening.

In my opinion, the phrases "investigate the *hwadu*" and "investigate the live word" in the above quotes should be altered to read "participate in the *hwadu*" and "participate in the live word." The Chinese character for "investigate" and "participate" is the same, so it is a matter of choice for the translator as to which word to use. I prefer "participate" as it helps to eliminate the dualistic subject/object dichotomy that is produced when we use the word "investigate." In other words, if one "investigates" the *hwadu*, he is maintaining a sense of separation between himself and the *hwadu*, whereas if he "participates" in the *hwadu*, he is acknowledging his unity with the *hwadu* right from the start. This initial understanding of inherent unity will immediately place him in the correct position, thus aiding him immensely in his practice.

It may also help us to understand Chinul's message more accurately if we can see that, contrary to the implication given by the words on the inscription quoted above, Chinul's life story may be viewed as epitomizing a continuous experience of being in a shipwreck. I have earlier emphasized the crucial importance of experiencing such a state. He underwent a severe struggle in order to reach enlightenment, and time and time again, after attaining a certain realization or understanding, he saw that it was not complete, and that he needed to continue on with his practice. When he arrived at the first gate, although he may have achieved a glimpse of recognition, he knew he had not yet reached his goal; similarly, upon reaching the second gate, he perceived that his struggle had not ended. It was only when he obtained his third awakening, arriving at the third gate, that he was able to claim, "[N]othing was stuck in my heart as an enemy from then on. I felt at ease and peaceful."[26] Thus, it is certainly not the case that Chinul lived peacefully and problem-free from one enlightenment experience to the next. Rather, it was only through encountering one difficulty after another, that is, from experiencing the feeling of being in one shipwreck after another, that he was able, through his own inner fortitude and diligent practice, to break through to an awakening.

Regarding the above-mentioned three gates, it should be pointed out here that although Chinul clearly viewed the *hwadu* gate as superior, he did not deny the value of the other two gates. In fact, he saw that one's entry into the first two gates is actually a prerequisite for entry into the third gate. As the practitioner moves from one gate to the next, he is manifesting a gradually maturing spiritual progress. Furthermore, the third gate itself helps to provide a deeper and truer meaning of the first two gates. In other words, through the use of *hwadu* practice, one's experience and understanding of both faith and wisdom become deepened. Thus, in order for the first two gates to become truly meaningful, the third gate must be included. Therefore, by emphasizing the primary importance of the *hwadu*, Chinul was enabling people to strengthen their own faith and wisdom.

The most important point for us to recognize is Chinul's own humanness, his unstated yet implicit struggle, as an ordinary human being, to attain the realization that all Buddhist practitioners seek: that there is an end to suffering, and that it is not apart from our daily lives. This realization, which took the Buddha six years (and countless previous lifetimes) to achieve, cannot be attained through faith or wisdom alone. According to Chinul, it can only be achieved when the mind is brought to a halt through the assiduous and often torturous practice of *hwadu* meditation, using the live word. It is this truth which has not been adequately conveyed in the inscription at Songgwam Monastery, and it is this truth which all Buddhist practitioners need to acknowledge and assimilate within themselves. The mind must be stopped. Armed with an understanding of this truth, a practitioner may save him/herself from pursing many dead-end paths and indeed may be well on the way to the goal.

Chinul's Views on Hwadu *Meditation*

In Chinul's text entitled "Resolving Doubts About Observing the *Hwadu*," he discusses the practice of *hwadu* meditation, stating that it can be pursued in two ways: (1) investigating the idea (which he calls the practice of the "dead word"), and (2) investigating the word (the practice of the "live word"). To use the dead word means, presumably, to use the mind to examine the question being studied. This is seen by Chinul as an inferior method of practice since the meditator has not let go of his conceptual approach and thus still functions within the realm of ideas and thoughts. Chinul clearly prefers the practice of the live word, in which the meditator examines the question through his conscious awareness only, to which thoughts are not permitted access. Chinul's views concerning these two approaches are made clear in the following passage:

> Those nowadays whose doubt has disintegrated have, for the
> most part, investigated the idea but not the word. . . . When

these people use their minds in meditation they still retain views and learning, understanding, and conduct. They are no better than those scholar-monks of today who are attached to words and letters and, in their contemplation practice, speculate that internally the mind exists but still search externally for truth. The subtler their search for truth becomes, the more they become subject to the defect of grasping at external signs. How can their approach be discussed in the same breath with that of men who have investigated the word, broken the doubt, had a personal realization of the one mind, displayed *prajñā*, and engaged in wide propagation of the teachings of Buddhism?[27]

Thus far, we are given a clear indication of the higher priority Chinul placed on the practice of the live word. However, when we look at the next few sentences, we encounter what seems to be a contradiction of Chinul's view. Let's read the following:

Those who have manifested such realization-wisdom [that is, those who practice the live word] are seldom seen and heard of nowadays. Consequently, these days we should value the approach which investigates the idea of the *hwadu* and thereby produces right knowledge and vision.[28]

The last sentence in this passage seems to belie what Chinul previously stated about the value of practicing the live word. This translation suggests that since it is much more difficult to practice the live word, we should support those who merely practice the dead word (i.e., the "idea" of the *hwadu*), as at the very least it affords them "right knowledge and vision." In my opinion, Chinul has made his position clear, in earlier passages of this chapter, concerning his preference for the live word over the dead word. Therefore, I can only conclude that the translator has erred in his translation of this passage. The important thing for us to understand is the supreme value Chinul placed on the live word, that is, using the *hwadu* without the crutch of intellectualization.

Chinul's "Enemy"

In the inscription on the stele at Songgwam Monastery, Chinul states that he had been living with an inner "enemy" his entire life, and that it was not until his third and final enlightenment experience that he no longer felt the presence of this enemy. The two terms he used were: (1) *yŏsu dongso*, or "staying with an enemy," and (2) *subul dongso*, or "the enemy is no longer there." In examining these two radically contrasting terms, we need to ask several questions. First of all, did Chinul intend to say that his previous two enlightenment experiences did not help in eliminating the enemy? If that were the case, then we could not truly call them enlightenment experiences, but merely some type of initial awakening. Secondly, how are we to interpret his statement that after the third enlightenment the enemy had disappeared?

With regard to this second question, it is important that we not misunderstand his meaning. Our tendency as ordinary, unenlightened beings is to mystify the enlightenment experience and view it as some magical, otherworldly state, similar to Jesus Christ's description of the kingdom of heaven. Yet do we really know what the Buddha experienced when he attained enlightenment? Do we understand or have access to his inner state? Certainly his understanding was transformed, but what does that mean? Was he suddenly transported to a world of never-ending bliss?

Although Chinul's words on the inscription may be seen as those of a victorious warrior, they may also be seen as those of a defeated soldier. Chinul confessed very humbly that he had lived with an enemy inside of him for his entire life. We need to recognize the significance of this statement, and its relevance for our own lives as well. It is this statement that makes Chinul's story a religious one; it is his humble confession that makes us identify with his failure and help us to see what an immense struggle is involved in confronting this enemy. Chinul's story is essentially an ongoing experience of being in one shipwreck after another, as mentioned in the previous section. To view his life in this way should help us not only to feel empathy for his struggle but should also provide us the courage and faith with which we can face our own difficulties.

Yet we need to realize, too, that the concept of conquering or defeating the enemy is an incorrect, dualistic way of understanding the final conclusion of such a struggle, that is, the enlightenment experience itself. Enlightenment, whether it be Chinul's experience or our own aspiration, is not some mythological state in which the enemy has disappeared forevermore. Rather, it is a recognition, a realization, that our own understanding of the enemy has become incorporated within us to the extent that we no longer view the enemy as an enemy. This is the understanding that occurred at the Buddha's enlightenment—that at the time of such an enlightenment, all dualities vanish. Thus, there will no longer exist any perception of opposition, such as friend and enemy, good and bad, like and dislike, and so forth. This is what is meant by transformation.

With regard to Chinul, we know that following his final enlightenment experience, he began to venture forth from the monastery where he had been residing and started giving dharma talks to various groups of lay practitioners. Certainly, through his many encounters with all sorts of people, he must have understood that the "enemy" never permanently disappears. However, what undoubtedly did disappear was his own sense of antagonism or separation with regard to the enemy. He was thus able now, for the first time in his life, to make peace with the enemy, seeing it as an unavoidable part of himself, so that it no longer caused him to suffer.

Again, this is what the Buddha discovered: that all states abide within us, both positive and negative; we do not exist apart from any one of them. They can never be eliminated because they exist as a part of who we are. Thus we have the well-known Buddhist saying, "Nirvāṇa is saṃsāra, and saṃsāra is nirvāṇa." In the Heart Sūtra, one of the most often quoted sūtras, it is stated, "Form is emptiness, and emptiness is form." The word *form* may be understood to include all phenomena, including our own thoughts and feelings. To say that they are all "empty" is not to say that they don't exist, but rather that they have no identity of their own. Instead, they are participants in an all-inclusive, interdependent universe. They do have existence, but we need not experience them as painful if we are able to see that they all belong within this vast, unending realm of interconnection. Furthermore, according to the Buddha's teachings, these states and forms are not only interdependent but impermanent as well; thus, they can and will change.

So let's be careful and not misinterpret Chinul's words concerning the "enemy." This "enemy" exists eternally within each and every one of us, according to our position within the overall scheme of dependent origination. With diligent practice, as well as a certain amount of intellectual understanding, we can begin to correctly perceive our true relationship to this "enemy." We can begin to understand that it is not a heavenly realm that we should seek, but rather the realization that heaven and hell are not opposites. The enlightenment experience can show us that they are co-participants in the ongoing drama of life. Hell can never be entirely eliminated forever, and we cannot live in an eternally blissful state, yet these two extremes can, and will, upon enlightenment, coexist within us peacefully. Then, as was the case with Chinul, our suffering can and will end.

CH'AN AND TAOISM

Many scholars in the field of Asian philosophy and religion feel that the Zen (Chinese: Ch'an) sect of Buddhism represents a hybrid between Indian Buddhism and Chinese Taoism. They claim that Ch'an has an Indian father, as influenced by Buddhism, and a Chinese mother, as derived from Taoism. The father, Buddhism, is seen as the seed, or the original teaching, whereas the mother, Taoism, is the fertile soil within which the seed has grown.

This approach to Ch'an is correct as far as it goes, but it is important for us to realize that it reflects a *momjit*, or dualistic, understanding only. Its limitation is that it neglects the fundamental essence of Ch'an, which is its *mom*, or all-inclusive, nondual aspect. In terms of outward appearance or manifestation, the concept of having an Indian father and a Chinese mother may be viable, but in terms of the essence of the true reality, how much real significance does such a perspective have?

During the Tang and Sung dynasties in China, certain Buddhist practitioners developed what may be called a "protesting spirit" toward the traditional, *momjit*-oriented approach to spiritual practice which was prevalent at the time. They began to challenge their own *momjit* culture, in which language and scriptures were given the highest priority. By means of language, scriptures had been written, dogmas had been formulated, doctrinal schools had been created, and so forth. These scriptures, dogmas, and schools had all been originally developed in order to help free people from the limitation of their *momjit* culture. Yet because many practitioners became attached to these scriptures, dogmas, and schools, they were not freed not all, but remained entangled in the snares of *momjit*, the outward appearance. They were still unable to break through to the *mom*, the essence of Ch'an. The originators of the "protesting spirit," who were enlightened monks themselves, realized these people's predicament, and in accordance with their own innate understanding, they took things a step farther: they burned the scriptures, destroyed the Buddhist statues, eliminated the Buddha halls, and made such statements as, "If you see the Buddha, kill him!" How are we to understand these actions?

In both Ch'an and Taoist texts there often appear terms such as "no-thought," "no mind," "emptiness," "voidness," and so forth. Superficial interpreters of these terms simply comment that they represent the aspect of Ch'an that is symbolized by the Chinese mother, and leave it at that. However, such a cursory attitude does not adequately reflect the deep significance of these terms. By their casual understanding, these interpreters are totally disregarding the essence, or *mom*, of Ch'an. For those who investigate the matter thoroughly, it may surely be seen that in Ch'an there are two vital issues that must not be overlooked. The first is faith. Many people ignore the supreme role faith plays in Ch'an practice. In doing so, they are exposing their own lack of deep reflection, which can only arise through serious practice. What is faith? As we have discussed earlier, one of its meanings is that it is reflected in a complete acceptance of the word of the teacher. In Ch'an, the role of the teacher is seen as fundamental.

Ch'an practitioners assert that without a teacher, one cannot practice properly. Yet we may ask the question: Who is the right teacher? The ultimate answer is: the Buddha himself. In the Ch'an view, the Buddha is understood as existing everywhere, including within each and every one of us. Those of the Judeo-Christian tradition similarly claim that God is omnipresent, abiding within believers and nonbelievers alike, eternally supporting and guiding us all. Without an unwavering faith in such an all-abiding presence, is it possible for one to maintain a proper spiritual practice?

The second crucial issue with regard to Ch'an practice is the message inherent in the dependent origination theory. As mentioned previously, this theory, which is a main tenet of Hua-yen philosophy, maintains the understanding that all phenomena, including one's own thoughts, speech, and actions, arise from a previous source and act as seeds for the sprouting of future phenomena. Thus, there is nothing that arises or abides independently; each and every single thing in the universe is "dependent" upon something else. This theory helps us to better comprehend the Buddhist ideal of nonduality, for if all things are connected through dependent origination, how can they oppose or be separate from each other? The followers of both Hua-yen and Ch'an believe that as long as faith is present, then practice, too, is present, as the two do not exist apart from each other in duality, but are rather two parts of one whole. In other words, faith is not merely a mental concept but rather a living, vital energy. As soon as faith is affirmed, then immediately practice is seen to be operating as well. In terms of logic, it would seem that faith must come first; that is, one begins with faith and then, as a result of his faith, he begins to practice. However, in the Ch'an approach, practice is advocated first. Yet through the very action of practice, one may see that it is operating as a natural function of his faith. Thus, we may say that practice is the *momjit*, or the function of faith, while faith is the *mom*, or essence of practice. The two operate as two inseparable parts of a vast, unnamable whole. At this point we may need to ask: What is meant by practice? Practice is nothing other than a spontaneous and all-abiding compassion, both for oneself and for all sentient beings. When dualistic thinking occurs, compassion is often absent, but in the nondual realm compassion is always there. This understanding is reflected in the Buddhist practice of gathering together in a *saṃgha*, or group of practitioners, who meet to study and meditate on the Buddhist teachings. By their very presence in such a group, these practitioners are exhibiting the qualities of both compassion and nonduality.

What exactly is dualism? When the Buddha attained enlightenment, his first words were, "I found the Middle Way." He was continually warning people to avoid the two extremes, as they represent a dualistic way of thinking. The two extremes manifest as opposites: love and hate, joy and sorrow, pain and pleasure, and so forth. Dualistic thinking itself relies on language. We rely primarily on words and concepts; these in turn foster our conditioned habits, causing us to function in a preconceived and imbalanced manner. This way of thinking may be referred to as a "grooved consciousness"; our minds constantly run along a particular groove of conditioned thought. Thus, in any given situation, we tend to act in a way that accords with how we have habitually acted in past situations, rather than responding spontaneously and naturally to the needs and requirements of the present moment. When the Buddha urged people to avoid the two extremes, he was referring, in his own way, to this grooved consciousness. If this conditioned way of thinking is eliminated through deep reflection or meditation, then one's mind can function properly in the present, and is not dictated to by past memories or future wishes.

The crucial point here is to give up the analytical mind, allowing yourself to return to *mom*, to God. Let God do the thinking; let the consciousness of *mom* do the work. Don't hold on to your grooved consciousness. By doing so, you will have successfully penetrated to the natural, all-abiding essence of Ch'an.

CONFUCIANISM

Most people view Confucianism as a very pragmatic, political, down-to-earth system of thought. Confucius rarely talked about the heavenly realm; his primary concern was human society. Is there any way we can find a correlation between Confucianism and the unseen world of *mom*? First of all, let us take a look at what I feel is the most predominant aspect of Confucian thought. For many scholars involved with the study of Far Eastern philosophy, the main current running through all Confucian teachings is the concept of *jen*, which means compassion. Yet in the mid-1970s a small but important book was published by Dr. Herbert Fingerett, a professor of religious studies at the University of California at Santa Barbara. In this book Dr. Fingerett refuted such an emphasis on *jen* and asserted instead that it is *li*, which means propriety or ritual, that serves as the vital thread connecting all Confucian teachings. I feel that Dr. Fingerett touched upon a very crucial understanding of the *mom/momjit* paradigm. Why does this term *li* hold such great significance?

If we look at the Chinese ideogram for *li*, we note that, as is often the case with Chinese ideograms, it is made up of two separate characters. The one on the left represents a table used in a ritual offering, and the one on the right means "abundant harvest." The meaning as a whole, then, is the offering of a ritual in thanks for an abundant harvest. In ancient times, such a ritual was performed as a way of showing respect to the gods. Before the ritual occurred, certain preparatory steps were usually taken, such as cleansing of the body through washing and donning clean clothes, a purification of the mind through meditation, and the performance of a certain number of prostrations in front of the ritual table. Afterward, food and wine were usually offered as a further manifestation of thanks.

This was the original meaning of *li*. However, as the world grew larger and more complex, this term came to signify the various types of human relationships that existed. These relationships were viewed as being extremely important in terms of both the well-being of the people involved as well as the smooth functioning of the society as a whole. It was understood that all of these relationships needed to be conducted from a foundation of mutual love and cooperation. The term *li*, then, represented such a relationship, one that reflected the care and concern shown by each party for the other. For example, in the relationship between parents and children, the parents should not only love and care for their children, but the children should in turn show filial piety, or respectful obedience, to their parents. *Li*, then, reflected the harmonious manifestation of such a relationship. An equally important relationship, one that also required the cultivation of mutual love and respect, was that between the ruler of a state or nation and his subjects, the citizens of that state. In order for a king or emperor to be viewed by the people as fair and benevolent, he had to do a good job in taking care of them. The ruler was considered the "Son of Heaven," and as such, was required to embody the principle of the heavenly realm, which existed beyond the boundaries of his earthly domain. Thus, the ruler needed to be acquainted with Heaven's intentions. Needless to say, this was not always an easy matter for him to discern correctly.

Another vitally significant relationship as viewed by the ancients was that of siblings. After the parents, a child's brothers and/or sisters are usually his initial means of contact with other human beings. As such, they most often represent the child's first experience of opposition or frustration with regards to his own desires. Even at this early stage of his life, he must learn how to communicate his needs effectively. He will, hopefully, discover that he can do this more easily by restraining his own initial impulses and coordinating them with the needs and desires of those around him. A certain hierarchical order among the siblings was seen as crucial in helping this process to run smoothly; thus, the eldest took care of the one born right after him, who in turn tended to the next in line, and so forth. This practice of reciprocity, in which each cared for the other, was seen in these ancient times as vital, not only in dealings among siblings, but in all relationships. Other important relationships included that between husband and wife, between neighbors, and between friends. In all of these relationships, a certain order between the two parties was observed. This order was reflected in the various rituals that were performed on such occasions as holidays, birthdays, marriages, deaths, and so forth. These rituals were all enacted with the intention of maintaining smooth and harmonious relationships, and as such were representative of the meaning of *li*. As we all know, such an intention is not merely the reflection of an ancient custom; rather, *li* is practiced everywhere. It is just as important in our modern times as it was hundreds of years ago for people to care for each other, and to exhibit compassion in times of need.

Interestingly, one of the most effective means of creating harmonious relationships is through the use of repetition. It may be seen that very often a relationship may be deepened through the practice of one or both parties exhibiting the same behavior over and over again. The very first sentence spoken by Confucius, in his *Analects*, states, "Is it not a pleasure to learn and to repeat or practice from time to time what has been learned?"[30] The Chinese ideogram for practice, called *shih*, has two parts, one situated above the other. The one on top means "the wings of a bird." For a bird, flying is its means of survival; without its wings it cannot fly. In order to fly, it must flap its wings over and over again, without stopping. The bottom character means "to say"; thus, the overall meaning of "practice" as depicted by this symbol is to repeat the saying of something again and again, like a baby bird learning how to fly. At first, of course, the bird will fail, but if he doesn't give up, eventually he will learn how to do it. The important thing is the repetition. With repetition you can make something your karma. Accumulated habits, acquired through repetition, become karma and are not changed so easily. This is the way, then, that smooth and harmonious relationships can be created and developed.

Now let us return to our discussion of *mom*. What is the correspondence between the creation of harmonious relationships and the invisible realm of *mom*? It is simply this: as we have learned, *mom* is considered the essence, the fundamental basis upon which the entire phenomenal realm is governed. Similarly, nothing is more essential, more basic, and more fundamental than human relationships. Although we may raise the act of abstract thought to the status of a god, still it cannot be denied that no matter how much thinking we do, we inevitably must return to reality by way of our daily lives of interaction with others. Usually our primary relationships are with other members of our immediate family; this is why they are given so much importance in Confucian teachings. In reality I am a husband, a father, a son, a neighbor, a faculty member, and so forth. It is crucial that if my life is to run smoothly, my thinking and my relationships must be harmonized. If I fail in this, it is because my thinking has not properly conformed itself to my dealings with others. In the past, when I was a young man, my thinking and my reality did not fit together well, so I ended up becoming a monk. In today's world, we witness the existence of gangsters, dropouts, and monastics, to give just a few examples. Yet these individuals are an exception to the norm; most people center their lives around their home and family.

Confucianism is the one philosophical system that pays deep attention to this area of life, that is, human relationships. Other philosophies or religions may address the issue, but Confucianism discusses it with the utmost constancy and profundity. This is one reason why Confucianism is not considered a religion. Also, unlike religions, it has no sanctuary or meeting place, such as a temple, mosque, or church. It has no priest, no scriptures, and no dogma with which to control people. These types of structures are created by human beings due to their own limitations. Unfortunately, what usually begins to happen after these structures have been established is that the group itself, rather than the teachings, becomes the predominant influence and concern. The smooth functioning of the group becomes of such paramount importance that anyone who questions or disagrees with the group's standards is ostracized. Issues of truth, honesty, human rights, justice, and so forth, all become subordinated to the theme of the group's prosperity. Any action, even if it is a virtuous one, is punished if it is seen to infringe on the security and cohesiveness of the group. In my opinion, the group represents the beginning of evil. Yet this is the age of groups of all kinds. Our own country consists of a group of states called the United States. The strongest impulse of any group is not religious; actually, religions arose in order to combat this human tendency. Sadly, though, organized religions also exhibit the same exclusive and hierarchical tendencies as any other group.

In Confucianism, there is no group system; rather, the home is the sanctuary and the family members are the clergy. Some people see Confucianism as a failure because it lacks a dogma, a priest, a sanctuary, and so forth. In my view, however, this makes Confucianism a success. In Korea, almost all religious people, no matter what religion they believe in or adhere to, are Confucians first. Thus, they may be Confucianized Buddhists or Confucianized Christians, but they all fundamentally believe in the Confucian ideals of compassion, respect for others, and harmonious relationships. The visible system of Confucianism may have disappeared, but its teachings are practiced everywhere.

In the fifteenth to the twentieth centuries in Korea, during which the Chosŏn dynasty reigned, Confucianism was the dominant belief system and Buddhists were persecuted for their beliefs. Buddhist monks were not even permitted to enter the capital city. As a reaction to this, an anti-Confucian group emerged and began to exhibit a certain amount of influence. Yet ironically, even the members of this group were unable to avoid practicing the basic Confucian ideals of compassion and respect for the other members. I find it very interesting to observe that in the case of Confucianism, the system itself has disappeared, as I noted above, yet its teachings are still widely practiced. On the other hand, the systems of both Buddhism and Christianity are very much in evidence, but it is a sad fact that although their ideals are expressed with great vigor, they are rarely practiced according to the spirit in which they were created.

It is a similar case with Pure Land Buddhism. In Korea, Pure Land Buddhism has never become successful as an independent order. To this day there is no specific Pure Land order or organization in Korea. This is very different from the situation in Japan, where Pure Land is the most powerful Buddhist order. Interestingly, despite the fact that there is no Pure Land order in Korea, most Korean Buddhists perform the Pure Land practice of chanting *yŭmbul*, which is homage to Amida Buddha. In Japan, however, the Pure Land order and the Zen order are kept separate. Thus, Zen practitioners do not usually chant this homage to Amida Buddha (called *nembutsu* in Japanese), nor do Pure Land believers practice the various forms of Zen meditation. Yet in Korea, where there is no Pure Land order, everyone recites Buddha's name very comfortably!

The conclusion that I draw from this is that non-being does not always mean non-being, and being is not always being. As another example, there is a Nobel Prize for science, yet there is no Nobel Prize for mathematics, even though science could not exist without mathematical laws and functions. We can see, then, that real existence does not exist simply as a form of visible existence; it is rather an existence without form. This brings us back to our discussion of *mom*. Real existence is best understood as *mom*; it is most appropriately viewed as existing beyond our senses and mind.

In Korea, because of persecution by the government, the Zen order of Buddhism was discontinued for hundreds of years. It wasn't until the early twentieth century that a monk named Kyung-huh revived it. Under his tutelage many authentic Zen masters began to emerge and a lineage was created that continues to this day. However, Kyung-huh himself eventually disappeared from the order. Later, his disciples discovered his corpse in a desolate area of northern Korea, near the Manchurian Peninsula. They found out from the people of the village where his body was discovered that he had been teaching Confucian classics to children of the village.

What does this mean? Did Kyung-huh betray Buddhism by becoming a Confucian teacher? Did he himself convert to Confucianism? I think we need to view the situation a bit differently. Far from betraying the Buddhist ideal, he was actually fulfilling it. The most fundamental theme in Zen is: be a human being, right here and right now. This is dogma-free and system-free; it is indeed independent of all restraints. This was exactly how Kyung-huh was living. He was teaching children how to be true to themselves by thinking, speaking, and acting as respectful and compassionate human beings. We need to find a way of thinking and living that lies beyond a church-oriented or dogma-oriented philosophy, as such philosophies tend to idealize and idolize their leaders, namely, Buddha, Christ, and so forth. As long as one functions on such a level, that is, of imitation, the Buddhist way cannot be practiced successfully. In my view, Kyung-huh lived as a man of *mom*. Confucianism is often seen as a teaching of *momjit*, yet its real intention is to help us return to our true status as human beings, or persons of *mom*. When that is accomplished, one performs whatever is needed by the *mom* of the moment. Yet in such an act, there is no attachment. This is the true meaning of Confucianism, yet it is discerned by very few.

CHAPTER FOUR

Present-Day Applications

LETTER AND NON-LETTER CULTURE/ONE MIND

It is universally recognized that language, and the use of words, plays a vital role both in our individual lives and in the functioning of our society as a whole, whether it be East or West. Without the use of words, we would not only be helpless in terms of carrying out all the myriad details of our present-day existence, but we would also be rendered equally incapable of learning about our past history or of investigating into our future concerns and needs. Yet in actuality, the letter itself, the alphabet, was invented only a mere five thousand years ago. That is really not such a long time, considering the fact that humans have existed on this planet for a far greater length of time. Thus, if we divide human civilization into two parts, one that existed before the invention of the alphabet, which I have termed "non-letter culture," and the other which arose and developed subsequent to the creation of the alphabet, or "letter culture," we can see that the former civilization was in existence for a far longer period of time than the latter. If we think about it, this realization has extraordinary implications. How is it that we have become so dependent on the use of the written word in such a comparatively short period of time?

Yet even though it is quite obvious that we now live in such a letter culture, how many hours a day do we actually spend in speaking, writing, or making use of words in some way (such as reading or watching TV)? Certainly, there are large periods of time within the framework of a day in which we are not operating from such a cognitive level. If we reflect about this, we may realize that the existence of a non-letter orientation still abides in our lives. We know that our brain primarily performs a rational, logical, and analytical function—one that has been determined by scientists to operate from the left side of the brain. At the same time, we all know that this is not the only aspect of human consciousness, that there also exists an intuitive, nonlinear framework, which originates from the right side of the brain and is equally important for our individual as well as our collective well-being. It is to meet the needs of this aspect of consciousness that the various religions and metaphysical systems have been created and pursued since the beginning of civilization.

Now I would like to expand our understanding of letter and non-letter culture. In an earlier chapter we discussed Wŏnhyo's commentary on the first chapter of *The Awakening of Mahāyāna Faith*. There we saw that in this text Aśvaghoṣa discusses at length the unifying and comprehensive concept of One Mind, which I have termed *mom*. He defines One Mind as "the Mind of the sentient being,"[1] further stating, "This Mind includes in itself all states of being of the phenomenal world and the transcendental world."[2] Thus, it may be said to be the Absolute, or *mom*, from which all else arises. As we saw earlier, he describes this One Mind as containing within it two aspects, the absolute and the relative (or phenomenal). These two aspects may be seen to play a role in our lives similar to the above-mentioned qualities of a letter and non-letter culture. Just as both of these attributes, which we may label intuition and reason, reside within us, so do the absolute and relative aspects of One Mind also abide within our consciousness. We embody many such dichotomies, whether or not we are aware of this at any given moment. For example, according to traditional Chinese teachings, all existence is comprised of the varying fluctuations of yin and yang (or light and dark, passive and active, and so forth). In a more contemporary vein, the field of psychology informs us that we all inherently possess both male and female characteristics.

Language is a very useful tool to help us understand the relative aspect of existence. The Chinese character for the word *relative* translates as "both arising and ceasing." We may further define it as referring to the activity of birth and death, thus embodying the principle that everything that appears (or arises) will eventually disappear (or cease) with the inevitable passage of time. In Buddhism, all *dharmas*, or "things" that make up the universe, are divided into two categories: conditioned and unconditioned. Conditioned *dharmas*, like the relative aspect of mind, all possess the characteristics of arising and ceasing; that is, they are all "conditioned," or subject to, birth and death. Unconditioned *dharmas*, on the other hand, are utterly free from such characteristics, as is the absolute aspect of mind. The state in which they abide is commonly called *nirvāṇa* (in Sanskrit). This may be seen as corresponding to another Sanskrit term, *ākāśa*, or space. Although all things that exist within space are subject to the constant activity of arising and ceasing, space itself is not bound by such conditions.

It should also be understood that conditioned *dharmas* do not merely consist of "things" or objects, but of states of consciousness as well, such as emotions and thoughts. All such states are completely dependent upon various causes and conditions for their existence. When the causes have ripened, they will appear; when the causes reach their ultimate fruition, they will accordingly disappear.

As is the case with *mom* and *momjit*, the absolute and relative aspects within us cannot be separated. Yet we should also look at the nature of the mind as a whole, or what Asvaghoṣa calls "One Mind." We have already said that it contains within it two aspects, absolute and relative. Yet the paradox here is that although it contains the relative, its fundamental nature is that of the absolute. To make the matter more complex, it would not be correct to say that its absolute nature is anything other than its relative nature, and vice versa. Thus, it may be seen to exist as both, and yet as neither, for it cannot be bound by any such verbal or conceptual descriptions. Similarly, from an ontological perspective, one dimension cannot be said to hold primacy over the other.

Mom, as we have previously discussed, may be approached in the same way. Even though it is referred to as absolute, it contains within it two aspects, which we earlier called the ordinary and the religious. We may also label these aspects as visible and invisible. We may begin to understand this more clearly through an investigation into the meaning of death, for at the moment of death the visible *mom* dies, along with the body, but the invisible *mom* does not die.

What is One Mind? It is the absolute *mom*, which is indescribable. Yet within it abide all the readily describable and nameable phenomena of the universe. In Christian terms, One Mind is God, who creates and contains all the creatures of existence. Within His Creation he abides as the Absolute, the unconditioned dharma, the *mom*. Jesus Christ was intuitively aware of this, and he often claimed that God exists within us. Similarly, in Buddhism, if there indeed is an external existence, then it must be located within all created things. The absolute aspect, then, may be seen as a vehicle of connection; we are each unavoidably an essential part of it.

STAGES OF PRACTICE

In attempting to understand *mom*, it is important that we not become attached to the word. As we pointed out earlier, *mom* can never be accurately comprehended by our conceptual mind. How can we access it then? We need some type of practice if we are to attain a deeper, more thorough understanding of its nature. Throughout our practice, however, we need to maintain the awareness that *mom* is never apart from us, not even for a millionth of a second. Such an awareness alone may be considered a very important form of practice. In a broader sense, we may divide our practice of understanding *mom* into three stages. (It may be added here that the same division may apply to the Christian practitioner as well.) The first stage entails a primarily passive level of participation in which one is initially absorbing various sources of information, such as listening to lectures and sermons or reading scriptures and sūtras. The next stage involves the ability to perceive *mom*/God as it/He abides in the universe around us. Thus, when we observe other people or scenes or nature we may begin to get a glimpse of the workings of another order of reality. The third stage concerns the ability to see *mom*/God operating within ourselves and all the mundane aspects of our daily lives. Awareness of *mom* or God by itself, however, is not considered the final stage as long as there still exists a sense of separation between the awareness and the one who is aware. Thus, to realize that *mom*/God is operating in all aspects of one's life is not to have arrived at the final stage of practice. The ultimate stage of realization is indeed an awareness, but in that awareness there exists no differentiation between subject and object, or perceiver and perceived. In the West, it is believed that it is only through God's grace that one may arrive at such a stage. In the East, however, the practitioner's individual efforts are seen as of crucial importance to the realization of unity with *mom*. In Eastern teachings, this is called the awareness of emptiness, and is viewed as the ultimate goal. Practice is usually viewed as vital if one is to attain this realization. Earlier, we delved more deeply into various issues involving practice.

In the final analysis, it is the seriousness and the capacity for commitment on the part of the student, which is heralded by a ripening of certain karmic conditions, that will determine his ability to work with a *hwadu* or engage in other practices in the search for *mom*. No one can know when the student will be ready. There is a story a contemporary Korean Zen master is fond of telling about the husband of one of his female students. This man willingly and faithfully drove his wife to the temple on a regular basis so that she could attend lectures there as well as engage in meditation practice. The husband himself had no particular interest in Buddhism and was content to wait for his wife in the car. On numerous occasions both the wife and the Zen master prevailed upon the man to at least come inside the temple and wait for his wife in the lobby, instead of isolating himself outside. Their efforts, however, inevitably proved fruitless. After this had been going on for some time, the Zen master finally took action; determinedly, he came out to the man's car one day, pulled the man out of the car, and pushed him into the temple. Succumbing to the master's will, the man agreed to sit in the lobby while his wife listened to a lecture. Sitting outside the lecture hall, patiently waiting for his wife, he could not help overhearing the words of the Zen master as he spoke to his students. He was discussing the *hwadu* that proclaims, "If you meet the Buddha on the road, kill him!" The man, upon hearing these words, was utterly shocked. Even though he felt that he himself was not a believer, still he knew of the deep respect with which the Buddha was held by his followers. What could the master possibly intend by espousing a teaching that endorsed the murdering of that very leader who was so greatly esteemed? The man was not merely puzzled, but rather felt confused to the point of utter incomprehension. He became so absorbed in the seeming conflict of ideas that the dilemma consumed his every moment of attention. It began to torment him not only during all of his waking hours, but at night as well, when he was trying to sleep. His life became one of tremendous, ongoing upheaval.

Now, it is evident to any practitioner of East Asian Buddhism that the man, whether willingly or not, had adopted this particular *hwadu* as his own, and had undertaken the intense practice of seeking its resolution, with a sincerity and dedication equal to that of any committed Buddhist. Eventually, he was able to reach a breakthrough in his understanding and to arrive at a solution to the apparent contradiction, so that when he approached the Zen master with the results of his efforts, he was indeed given a positive confirmation. What I find so fascinating about this story is that the man initially had no resemblance whatsoever to a seeker of truth, yet evidently his karmic causes and conditions had ripened to the point that he was quite prepared to face the exhaustive, transformative experience of spiritual practice as manifested in working with a *hwadu*. The spiritual path opened up naturally, right in front of him, and became the inevitable next step on his journey from birth to death.

In my view, two qualities are needed on the part of the practitioner in order for his practice to develop. The first is honesty with oneself, which means a basic understanding about who one is and what his life is all about. He may not be clear about his direction, but it is absolutely essential that he not attempt to deceive himself in any way. Otherwise, his spiritual efforts will be futile. The second quality necessary for spiritual practice is the ability to cultivate and maintain a basic respect for others, regardless of whether one agrees with their beliefs. These two qualities are a reflection of one's ability to further respect and cherish the greater gift of life, and the life force contained within it, that has been handed to each one of us at the moment of our birth into this unfathomable world.

The Raft

Earlier, we touched upon the saying that advises the practitioner to use the Buddhist teachings as a raft to carry him/her to the other shore. This far shore, which represents the enlightened state of the practitioner himself, is, ironically, not far away at all, but rather exists intrinsically within us. Yet until we have stepped foot on this shore, we remain blind to this fact. The additional instruction is given that we must abandon this raft, that is, the teaching, once we have arrived at our goal—or once we have at least reached that elusive shore. Just as the mature frog is able to cast off his previous identity as a tadpole, and just as the beautiful butterfly is no longer an ugly caterpillar, so we, too, become transformed through our practice into beings who bear little, if any, resemblance to our original state. Yet although a radical transformation has indeed occurred, there still will remain some slight connection, some minute, almost imperceptible continuity, between the old state and the new one. An analogy might be the comparison of the qualities of a child with those of his parents. Does an offspring, even upon becoming a mature adult, ever completely eliminate or throw off all the characteristics that he has inherited merely by being born into a particular family? It is highly unlikely; therefore, it is doubtful that the raft is ever completely abandoned. Certainly, however, we will no longer depend on it in the same way once we become enlightened. Rather, it may continue to serve as a valuable reference or departure point, reminding us of who we are.

Faith Revisited

Although the issue of faith has traditionally been less emphasized in Buddhism than in other religions, it is now increasingly being seen to be of great benefit to anyone who has the need and capacity to abide firmly within its boundaries. Although we examined this issue in depth in a previous section, I would like to add a few words here.

What is the nature of Buddhist faith in particular? In my opinion, one's faith should relate directly to the enlightenment experience of the Buddha himself. Our journey of faith must begin with our reflection on the Buddha's transformative realization that every sentient being is already perfectly enlightened. To have faith implies the ability, which is really just the willingness, to accept such an understanding, even though we have not yet experienced this truth for ourselves. Thus, it is of primary importance that we begin with the understanding that what we are searching for exists within our very being. The Diamond Sūtra tells us that if we are seeking something that we can apprehend with our senses, that is, something with a name or a form (Sanskrit: *nāma* or *rūpa*), then we will undoubtedly fall into the path of heretics and thus render impossible all attempts to discover the *tathagatha*, the enlightened one. Many people ignore this warning and instead pledge their allegiance to externals of all kinds. Even many spiritual leaders devote much of their time and energy in matters involving appearance. This leads not to freedom, but to further attachment and suffering. If one believes that appearance has any effect on his ability to become enlightened, he is betraying his faith in the quest for such a goal. To have faith refers to one's deepest conviction concerning the inner, hidden realm of *mom*; outward appearance holds no position of influence whatsoever.

Daily Practice

I would define practice as any karmic expression that brings me closer to the Buddha's teachings and to an enhancement of my own faith. In this I differ from those who insist on the necessity of regular meditation practice. I believe that even lying on your bed, staring up at the ceiling, and reflecting on the words of the Buddha can be a very effective way to practice. As long as one's thinking is clear, his verbal expressions as well as his actions will be greatly benefited. To believe that the practice of meditation by itself will eventually lead to enlightenment is to commit a grave error in understanding, for such a belief automatically establishes a dualism between the meditator and his goal. As we have already ascertained, no such duality exists; *mom* is already inherently within us. Therefore, if we do choose to undertake the practice of meditation, we need to clearly discern our reasons for doing so. As discussed earlier, if it is for the purpose of attaining enlightenment, then we are already far from understanding the true nature of reality.

The Unknown Factor

One of the biggest mistakes we can make in our practice is to be attached to *momjit* due to our misunderstanding about its nature. *Momjit* is always momentary; it is impermanent. Yet many people believe that they can achieve greater clarity and understanding in their lives by amassing large collections of material from the *momjit* realm, such as the accumulation of knowledge. Does the possession of such a collection of data lead to wisdom? In my opinion, it merely creates a great storehouse of *momjit* material, and nothing else. Far from bringing us wisdom, this can actually become a tremendous burden for us. Something else is necessary if we are to attain wisdom; we need to tap into the unknown factor of *mom* (or God), which we are often very reluctant to do.

This matter was similarly addressed by an eminent sociologist, Émile Durkheim. He made the perhaps self-evident assertion that although any society is comprised of many individuals, the society itself cannot be defined by merely defining the individual alone. Society is made up not only of individuals but of another indescribable, unknown factor as well. This factor is a question mark—what is it? It is not something we can apprehend or express with our senses. Although Durkheim's approach was scientific, he may also be viewed as a theologian, for he realized that separation from this unknown factor of existence is impossible.

Christian theology also discusses this issue, proclaiming that it is not correct for us to attempt to understand God using our familiar, ordinary manner of thinking. God has created us—how then can it be possible for us to believe that we can understand Him on our own terms? We should instead always be asking ourselves (if we are of the Judeo-Christian tradition), "Who, really, is God?" He is an unknown; this fact should always be kept at the forefront of our practice. Similarly, in terms of *mom* and *momjit*, we don't know what *mom* is, and therefore need to approach its understanding with the utmost caution and respect.

It is perhaps for this reason that Neo-Confucians, such as T'oegye (Korea: sixteenth century) and Chu Hsi (China: twelfth century) were reluctant to accept the existence of God. They mentioned a "heavenly principle," but did not expand this further into an acknowledgment of personified Being. They maintained rather that the primary consideration should be the human being, but that to understand ourselves we need to first comprehend the heavenly principle. Why? Because we ourselves are a product of this heavenly principle. Thus, understanding the heavenly principle affords us a way to understand ourselves. Yet people run into difficulties when attempting to understand the heavenly principle. Its identity, like that of God or *mom*, is not so clear. What exactly is the heavenly principle? People often ended up abandoning their attempts to find an answer to this question, and found it easier to reverse the formula. Thus, they begin to claim that by first understanding the human being, the heavenly principle could be understood. This approach eventually led to much corruption, as people began to believe that they could attain the heavenly principle by means of their own limited human desires. Once again, they were attempting to define and identify *mom* through the limited and limiting manifestations of *momjit*, with disastrous results.

Desire

We need not condemn all human desires. Yet if our desires imprison us, so that we become materialists or hedonists, we will never find freedom. The basic understanding of Neo-Confucianism, before it became corrupted, is that despite our lack of understanding concerning the nature of the heavenly principle, we must realize that it, and not ourselves, is the proper governor of our desires. Therefore, if we can maintain our faith in this realization and in the heavenly principle itself, willingly yielding to its laws, then our desires will be appropriately channeled and our lives will be harmonious.

With regard to this, let us look at the behavior of a typical ten-year-old boy. It will not be possible for him to understand the words or actions of his parents for he has the mind of a child; he possesses neither significant experience nor depth of understanding. On the other hand, his parents, through their comparatively greater awareness, will have little difficulty in understanding their child. They themselves have already experienced and assimilated what he is now becoming familiar with for the first time. Similarly, a large container may be seen to easily accommodate having a smaller one put inside of it, yet a small container does not have the capacity of containing a larger one. Thus, we cannot hope to attain enlightenment (*mom*) through the limited perspective of our desires (*momjit*). It is only by allowing them to be transformed into a larger, more universal understanding and awareness that we may gain access to the realm of awakening. There is intrinsically no duality between desire and enlightenment, yet the higher realm cannot be approached through the lower one.

A valid question may arise at this point: If desire is contained within the larger realm of enlightenment, if it is indeed an integral aspect of the universe, why does it cause us such difficulty? Again, I believe it is a matter of how desire is approached. Let us look at the example of a newborn baby. When a child is born, the most important concern of the parents is to protect it from harm. They must initially perform all the necessary work required to keep it safe; eventually, they begin to teach it how to protect itself. This is what gives the child the notion of its own individuality and becomes its second karma, so to speak (its first karma, of course, is its birth). Yet when the child grows up to become a mature adult, he needs to shed this notion of individuality, just as a frog sheds its previous identity as a tadpole. Self-protection is no longer sufficient; something more is needed, a different logic altogether, which is the awareness and acceptance of the nondual nature of existence. In traditional cultures, this is considered the natural outcome of one's biological, organic development. In our modern times, however, children are not encouraged to grow up into mature, fully conscious adults. Rather, the self-protective stage is encouraged and prolonged, both by the parents and the society. Due to this, the sense of the individual's own unique importance is accordingly nourished. Thus, the majority of people living today are concerned with their own self-protection. It is only religion that advocates moving to a higher level through self-transformation. Within a religious context, the individual is still viewed as important, but the unknowable yet all-embracing factor, which we call God or *mom*, is recognized as holding even greater significance. Thus, according to the religious view, although our desires, manifested as *momjit*, are indeed a part of the universal *mom*, it is imperative for our own daily well-being as well as our spiritual growth that they be understood as *mom's* servants and not its masters.

THE FIVE STAGES OF PRACTICE ACCORDING TO CHINUL

In the philosophical and the religious system advocated by Chinul there are five stages of practice that lead to realization or enlightenment (which, for our purpose here, signifies the realization of *mom*). The first is a purely ethical stage, which involves following certain prescribed precepts, or moral guidelines for behavior. This may be considered as a necessary foundation for the practice and investigation of the following stages. The second stage is one of further purification, which occurs on a more inner level and which later practitioners have termed the Hīnayāna stage. It involves practices that specifically aim to refine one's awareness as manifested through his speech, thoughts, and actions. A key practice at the Hīnayāna stage is that of mindfulness. The third stage broadens the scope of practice so that one may begin to develop the understanding that essentially no separation exists between him/her and other sentient beings. This is commonly referred to as the Mahāyāna stage, and it is here that the Hua-yen teachings may find their abode. The highest level of understanding in the Hua-yen system is reflected in the phrase "*shih shih wu ai*," which roughly translates as "no obstacles or barriers between or among any phenomena whatsoever." We have already discussed Hua-yen theory in an earlier chapter. We may note here that it is this understanding of no separation that both inspires and enables the practitioner to summon up what is called the spirit of the bodhisattva. A bodhisattva, as mentioned earlier, is one who vows to delay his own final awakening or enlightenment in order that he/she may help others. Thus, one has moved beyond the limiting preoccupation with his own spiritual development and salvation, and has instead chosen to embody a larger, more universal view, in which he exists in complete unity with others. Thus, their liberation is equally as urgent as his own.

The fourth and fifth stages may both be considered as relating to the practice and understanding of Zen. The fourth stage refers specifically to all the teachings as propagated by the entire lineage of Zen masters. It involves the ability to analyze the message of Zen, which is basically the message of no separation, through one's intelligence. Chinul calls this using the "dead word"[3]; here the practitioner uses his rational understanding as a means of investigating the meaning or idea of a specific *hwadu* that he has been assigned by his master. A certain awakening is entirely possible here, yet the drawback of such a practice is that the bondage created by the presence and usage of one's intellect is not completely broken. The practitioner who reaches this stage may be termed one who is "enlightened through right understanding."[4] His practice is not considered complete, as he is unavoidably hampered by his intellectual understanding of the meaning of Zen (or the meaning of *mom*).

The fifth stage, however, frees the practitioner from all conceptual bonds; the key practice here is what Chinul terms the "live word."[5] One does not merely cogitate upon the idea or meaning of the *hwadu*, but instead radically focuses his attention on the key word itself, such as the word *mu* in the famous *hwadu* concerning the Buddha-nature of a dog. The promise of Zen is that if he faithfully and perseveringly concentrates on this word *mu*, without indulging in any speculative thoughts about what *mu* may signify, he will eventually be able to break through the barrier erected by his intellect and reach the final goal of "realization awakening."[6] This attainment epitomizes the end of all seeking; it is none other than the final, ultimate enlightenment. It is the fifty-second stage as described in the Hua-yen teachings, which may be arrived at only after one has passed through the previous fifty-one stages. Here the practitioner, through his diligent investigation of the live word, is no longer dependent upon what he has read, heard, or even previously experienced. All linguistic discourse is abandoned; all consciousness is eliminated. By the means of such a practice, no further obstacles to awakening remain.

It should be noted that when one enters the fifth stage of practice, this does not signify that he/she is now free from all suffering. A certain level of suffering may always remain; however, the practitioner's comprehension of his/her own suffering will be vastly different than that of someone at a lower stage. Chinul himself advocated the primacy of this stage, declaring that all the previous four stages have only limited value, for the practitioner of any of those lower levels is still inescapably bound by his own incomplete understanding. Only at the fifth stage is complete freedom realized.

PERSONAL STORY: APPLICATION OF THE
MOM/MOMJIT PARADIGM

At this point I would like to relate a personal story, which I feel aptly demonstrates how the *mom/momjit* paradigm may be successfully applied to the practical affairs of daily life. There is a certain relative of mine, a nephew, who lives in Korea; I will call him JK here, although these are not his real initials. Recently he sent me an e-mail stating that he would be coming to the United States for a week in the near future, and would like to pay me a visit. I immediately began to feel apprehensive, for the unhappy truth of the matter is that JK has been the source of much tension and aggravation for his family for a long time. Although he is married, with two or three teenage children, he has had a lengthy history of unemployment, and the burden of supporting the family has fallen entirely onto his wife's shoulders. Not only is he unstable in this regard, but he has a reputation for being a liar as well. Even in his e-mail to me, I felt that he was not being entirely truthful. He mentioned that he would be traveling to Boston, Houston, and Chicago, but it did not seem likely to me that he could adequately cover such a wide range of territory within the space of one week. Stating rather unceremoniously that he wished to

see my house, rather than expressing any particular desire to reac-
quaint himself with me or my wife, he merely asked for directions to
my home from Kennedy Airport. I sent him a polite but firm reply,
stating that I did not see how he could possibly do business in three
different American cities within a week's time, adding that I would
not be able to see him due to an already overcrowded schedule. He
responded immediately, saying that he would expand his stay to two
weeks and that he still intended to come. This quick reply indicating
a sudden change in his plans produced in me an even greater suspicion, and I felt more convinced than ever that he was not telling the
truth. This is not a business trip that he is making, I said to myself.
He undoubtedly wants to come to the United States in order to escape
from his miserable life in Korea. It is a known fact that no one there
trusts him; even his own wife does not dare to give him any money.
I decided not to answer his second correspondence.

Soon after this, I received two phone calls: first his sister phoned,
informing me of his departure date, and then a call came from his
mother, telling me that her son had now left Korea and asking me to
please take care of him here. I became both despondent and angry.
He didn't even have the courage to call me himself, I observed scorn-
fully. Both my wife and I felt extremely apprehensive over the whole
situation. As we discussed it together, the two terms that I kept using
to describe him were *kŏjit* and *hŭtjit*. The suffix *jit* means "behavior"
in Korean; various prefixes are then attached to it in order to refer to
particular types of behavior. For example, we are already familiar with
the term *momjit*; in this context, we might define this term as behavior
or actions that are derived from *mom*. As we have learned, *mom* itself
is a universal term; it would follow, then, that *momjit* may refer to any
and all behavior that a person may manifest. The words that I used
to criticize JK, however, refer to more specific or specialized modes of
behavior: *kŏjit* means to be false, deceitful, hypocritical, pretentious, and
so forth, while *hŭtjit* is a more expansive term which covers all illusory
or meaningless behavior. In using both of these terms to describe JK,
I was indeed covering a wide range of negative behavior.

However, suddenly in the midst of a particular lengthy and
vehement diatribe against him, I looked at myself and initiated the
following self-accusation: by criticizing JK in this way, are you not
perpetuating similar behavior? Perhaps you are not lying, but certainly
your thoughts and feelings are not helpful to this situation. Why don't
you approach the matter in a different way? If you could persuade
him to cease his *kŏjit* and *hŭtjit*, and instead perform *momjit*, what
would you suggest that he do?

The reader may also ask a very valid question at this point: If *momjit*, as we said above, reflects all behavior, then are not *kŏjit* and *hŭtjit* merely aspects of *momjit*? We must clarify here that although all appearances and thus all gestures and actions are said to be *momjit*, this term contains within it two categories or aspects: if the *momjit* that is manifested is operating from our good intentions or good will, then it may simply be called *momjit*. If, however, it is derived from false intentions or an evil will, then the ensuing behavior will be labeled *kŏjit* or *hŭtjit* or some other *jit*. Thus, I asked myself: How can JK cease doing *kŏjit* and instead do *momjit*? The answer seemed reasonably clear: he needed to confront me honestly and say: I want to stay in America, and I need your help. Since by the use of such words he would not be deceiving me in any way but would rather be directly and honestly stating his intentions, this would be an ad-mirable expression of *momjit*.

I then asked myself another question: In my criticism of him, am I doing *hŭtjit* or *momjit*? I was not so sure of the answer this time. I was well aware that I feared being placed in a disadvantageous posi-tion by his behavior, and therefore my feelings were not completely devoid of self-interest. Yet although I realized that I was not acting from *momjit*, I also felt that I had not deviated into the more danger-ous and unacceptable position represented by *kŏjit* or *hŭtjit*. Still, it bothered me that my behavior reflected a distortion of *mom* and could not, in good conscience, be called *momjit*. How can I perform *momjit* in this particular situation? I asked myself. As I mulled over this for awhile, what eventually came to my mind was the advice which Jesus Christ had given to his disciples on several occasions. In essence he said to them: Don't worry about yourself; God takes care of you. Let Him worry, that is His business. Immediately, I began to relax. I sought out my wife and said to her, "Both of us have been suffering because of JK's behavior. We have been trying to avoid experiencing any disadvantage to ourselves before he has even arrived. This is not right. A certain amount of trouble is unavoidable in this world, yet we have been choosing to suffer even before hell has appeared. If it is indeed our destiny to visit hell, we will not be able to escape, no matter how much worrying we do. So until that moment arrives, why don't we just live comfortably? If and when JK gets in touch with us, we can just be honest with him, telling him how much we can or can't help him. Let's just accept this situation and see how it progresses, and not attempt to avoid the possible suffering it may cause us." We both felt very comfortable with this resolution, and our anxiety abated.

Interestingly, to follow up on this story, he did arrive at my doorstep, unannounced, one day. However, I had told him in advance that I would be out of town and that was indeed the case. When he arrived, neither my wife nor myself were at home. He then proceeded to attempt to track me down via my office at the university, yet my secretary was not able to provide him with any further information. I did not hear from him upon my return home several days later.

However, I continued to question myself about the matter. What would Jesus or Buddha do in a similar situation? I wondered. I felt that they would probably not do anything special, and would just continue to maintain their faith. Buddha would have known that his Buddha-nature was protecting him, just as Jesus knew that God was always looking out for him. But I have a wife to support and a job to maintain, I reminded myself. The world in which I live is far different from that of Jesus' or Buddha's time. Is it really possible for me to just trust God completely and leave it at that? I felt that it was not. How, then, can I do *momjit*? I asked myself. I still could not resist this question. I began rising before dawn over the next few days, pondering the matter deeply and jotting down my questions and insights as they arose. My dilemma was this: I knew that I needed to trust *mom*, yet I felt that I could not. Is it impossible, then? I asked myself. Why are you trying to avoid personal disadvantage? In Confucian terms, this is the behavior of a small man. If you are indeed damaged by this episode, what kind of damage could possibly occur? What does it mean to have faith in *mom*? What kind of behavior is required here?

I felt at a loss as to how to proceed. Merely remonstrating with myself to have faith was not sufficient; it did not in itself enable me to do so. What finally helped me was the realization that returning to *mom*, which was essentially the same thing as having faith, did not mean that I first needed to abandon my ordinary consciousness. This would naturally occur once I accessed *mom*; thus, to abandon all language is an end in itself but should not and cannot be resorted to as a means to reach that end. In fact, what I needed to do initially was to make full use of my mental faculties in order to deeply investigate the situation. I realized that I had the entire realm of *momjit* at my disposal in order to help me do so. I recalled the three wisdoms of Buddhism: listening, thinking, and self-cultivation. Practitioners make use of these faculties in a progressive sense: by first listening, or initially becoming aware of all the ramifications of a particular situation, including all the various ways in which it may be handled, then thinking about the issue deeply, and finally turning inward to meditate or pray in order to detach themselves from all external distractions. The first two practices of listening and thinking certainly require that we make all possible use of language and conceptual consciousness, products of the world of *momjit*. It is only when we begin the process of self-cultivation, through meditation, chanting, or prayer that language and concepts are eliminated—though naturally and on their own, not forcefully—and we are finally allowed to enter the realm of *mom*. It is through such a process, I saw, that we are enabled to make the correct decisions, and to come up with fair solutions in terms of public justice. I realized that making progressive use of these three wisdoms was indeed an exemplary method which enabled one to return to *mom*; it successfully used *momjit* as a tool by which one eventually could first eliminate all *momjit* and in so doing, spontaneously enter the realm of *mom*, the realm of faith.

Final Thoughts on *Mom* and *Momjit*

"Why are you so attached to the *mom/momjit* paradigm?"

Various friends have asked me this question on several occasions. Instead of answering them directly, I ask them in turn, "What is your definition of the *mom/momjit* paradigm? If you understood it the way I do, you would want to study it further."

I am aware that some people are concerned about my ceaseless investigations into the complexities of this ancient East Asian philosophical/religious model. Yet I have a good reason for my relentless pursuit; this reason, in my opinion, cannot be ignored. It relates directly to the issue of religiosity in the human being. As I have already discussed this term in previous chapters, I will just briefly summarize some thoughts here.

In discussing religiosity, we must begin with the undisputed fact that every one of us is subject to suffering. Why do we suffer? Because of our inner conflict. What is the nature of this conflict? It centers around the fact that how we live our lives, through the projection of our thoughts, words, and deeds, is running contrary to an innate presence within us, which I am calling a "universal principle." Because of our inner conflict, these two seemingly opposing powers are colliding with each other. Our body operates automatically, through the functioning of this universal principle. Our desires, however, which function by means of the body, have somehow become diverted from this principle, and instead are maintained by various external man-made qualities, such as greed, anger, confusion, and so forth. It is the collision of these two forces within us that causes our suffering.

What is the solution to this dilemma? It is to somehow enable these two forces to move closer to each other and eventually become united. We need to remember that ultimately our behavior is not isolated from the innate, universal principle; all of our thoughts, words, and deeds have this principle as their source. If we can train ourselves to acknowledge and accept the presence of this universal principle throughout the myriad events of our daily lives, then we will be able to eliminate our suffering and attain peace. Our acceptance of the universal principle within us, and the ability to live our lives in accordance with it, is what I am terming "religiosity."

I can truly say that throughout the course of my lifelong study of this matter, I have found that the only Asian teaching that has addressed it adequately is the *mom*/*momjit* paradigm, or the *t'i-yung* construction, as it is better known. As the relation between *mom* (*t'i*) and *momjit* (*yung*) is seen to be one of nonduality, then we can also say that the relation between the two forces within us, that is, our innate bodily or universal principle (*mom* or *t'i*) and its many functions with all its desires (*momjit* or *yung*) is nondual. People tend to see these two forces as opposing each other, yet the one cannot exist without the other. They are both interdependent and inseparable, like two sides of the same coin.

Many people, however, either disagree with or do not fully comprehend the above understanding. For example, in 1960, Dr. Kenji Shimada, a professor of philosophy at Kyoto University, formally criticized the *t'i-yung* construction, claiming that it represents a "circular" logic and as such is not only impractical but confusing and irrational as well. His remarks were applauded by a majority of Japanese scholars, who then advocated for the elimination of the *t'i-yung* construction as an appropriate tool for philosophical inquiry.

In the early 1980s I asked a noted Stanford University professor of Buddhism how he teaches the *t'i-yung* construction. He replied that he does not teach it at all, as he felt that it would only cause confusion for his students. In my own experience, I have found that among the four PhD graduates who studied under me, only one has shown any real interest in or understanding of the *mom*/*momjit* paradigm.

Why do people have such a lack of regard for what I consider to be an outstanding model for the understanding of all existence? In the academic world, those who approve of it are viewed as either ignorant or else as idealistic dreamers, whereas those who scorn it are held in high esteem. Is this view correct? I do not believe so. Then where are these people going wrong? I would like to offer the following diagnosis.

First of all, in my opinion, the people who are criticizing *t'i-yung*, or *mom*/*momjit*, are holding a distorted view of *t'i*, or *mom*. By attaching themselves to the common, everyday, physical sense of the word *mom*, they are in actuality equating it with *momjit*, that is, as something that is changeable and impermanent. This is a serious mistake; those who are viewing *mom* in this way are not paying attention to its most vital and fundamental aspect, which is its nature of permanence, or *nitya*. Although *mom* is normally translated to mean the physical body, we should not make the mistake of solely confining ourselves to that definition. We need to keep in mind that the body itself, when discussed in terms of *mom*, has two aspects: permanent and impermanent. People tend to avoid accepting the permanent aspect of *mom*. They base their views on the understanding that Buddhism itself espouses *anitya* (impermanence) and not *nitya* (permanence). This teaching, however, represents the earlier Buddhist philosophy, known as Hīnayāna, and does not reflect the later, more expanded and inclusive Mahāyāna understanding. We need to recognize that it is the permanent aspect of *mom* that gives it such value.

Another reason for the misunderstanding of *mom/momjit* has to do with the fact that this paradigm is a simile—it is not, in and of itself, the final truth. It can be compared to the finger that acts as a pointer to the moon in the famous East Asian Buddhist metaphor. The truth, or the goal, is the moon itself, but people tend to focus all their attention on the finger, completely forgetting about that to which the finger is pointing. The simile itself, in this case the *mom/momjit* paradigm, is useless unless people are able to see beyond it and grasp the truth to which it is referring. The truth, or *upameya*, of the *mom/momjit* paradigm is the nonseparable relationship, that is, the nonduality, which exists between *mom* and *momjit*. Many of those who are objecting to the *mom/momjit* paradigm are actually objecting to the concept of nonduality itself.

What we need to understand is that this concept of nonduality is key to the understanding of *mom* and *momjit*. Most people do not realize the extent to which we are all trapped by the forces of dualistic thinking as a result of our unavoidable involvement with language and words. Language itself creates duality, as its purpose is to make distinctions, that is, to enable us to distinguish between all kinds of differing qualities, such as good and bad, yours and mine, and so forth. To a great extent we are held prisoners by language, just as we are held prisoner by our physical body. But let us think of God: His position is different—it cannot be explained away by the concept of dualism. Let us observe the fact that many of the qualities that we ascribe to Him are in themselves qualities of nondualism: omnipresent, omniscient, omnipotent, and so forth. What does this term *omni* mean? It means "all" or "existing everywhere," just like *mom*. Again, people fail to see this because they are so firmly entrenched within the confines of the linguistic system.

There is a story from the Tang dynasty in China about a Diamond Sūtra specialist who carried around on his back all sorts of commentaries relating to this sūtra. One day he met up with a Zen master who asked him, "If it is nighttime and I blow out the candle so that there is complete darkness, what will you see?" The specialist of course replied, "Nothing." The Zen master then asked, "And if I take away all your commentaries, then what can you tell me about the Diamond Sūtra?" The specialist was at a loss for words. As the story goes, the Zen master then beat the specialist with a stick, whereupon the specialist became enlightened.

Whether or not we believe that the events of this story actually took place, there is an important message here. Our concern here should not be the Zen master or the Diamond Sūtra specialist, but rather the issue of the flexibility of one's consciousness. If we are attached to our ideas, to our accomplishments, to our possessions, as the sūtra specialist was attached to his commentaries, then where is the benefit? No matter how wonderful or grandiose our material or intellectual attainments, if we do not possess a healthy, flexible state of mind, how can we be said to be free?

The value of the *mom/momjit* paradigm is that it directly points us in the direction of freedom, which lies in the understanding of the inherent nonduality of all existence. If we choose not to accept its message, then we are choosing to neglect a teaching that can help us open the door to a deeper understanding of life's mysteries. I cordially invite you, the reader, to open the door and welcome this beautiful and powerful message of nonduality into your hearts.

Notes

INTRODUCTION

1. D. T. Suzuki, *Studies in the Lankāvatāra Sūtra*, 230–36.

CHAPTER ONE. INITIAL CONSIDERATIONS

1. Please refer to "Nāgārjuna" in the glossary.

CHAPTER TWO. *MOM* AND *MOMJIT* AS TOOLS FOR TRANSFORMATION

1. Robert Buswell, *The Korean Approach to Zen*, 251.
2. Ibid, 250.

CHAPTER THREE. OTHER TEACHINGS

1. Peter H. Lee, *Sourcebook of Korean Civilization*, 157.
2. Ibid.
3. Ibid.
4. Ibid.
5. Ibid., 157–158.
6. Ibid., 158.
7. Ibid.
8. Ibid.
9. Robert Buswell, *Cultivating Original Enlightenment*, 47. Note: Buswell's translation, as follows, is slightly different from the *Sourcebook of Korean Civilization*, which I used: "Now, the fountainhead of the one mind, which is distinct from existence and nonexistence, is independently pure."
10. Ibid. Buswell's translation: "The sea of the three voidnesses, which subsumes absolute and conventional, is profoundly calm."

11. Ibid. Buswell: "Profoundly calm, it subsumes dualities and yet is not unitary."

12. Ibid. Buswell: "Independently pure, it is far from the extremes and yet is not located at the middle."

13. Ibid. Buswell: "Because it is not located at the middle and yet is far from the extremes, dharmas that are non-existent do not linger in nonexistence and characteristics that are not non-existent do not linger in existence."

14. Ibid. Buswell: "Because it is not unitary and yet subsumes dualities, those phenomena that are not absolute need not be conventional and those principles that are not conventional need not be absolute."

15. Ibid. Buswell: "Because it subsumes dualities and yet is not unitary, there are none of its absolute or conventional qualities that are not established and none of its tainted or pure characteristics that are not furnished therein."

16. Ibid. Buswell: "Because it is far from the extremes and yet is not located at the middle, there are none of the existent or nonexistent dharmas that are inactive and none of its affirmative or negative concepts with which it is not equipped."

17. Peter H. Lee, *Sourcebook of Korean Civilization*, 145–46.

18. Red Pine, *The Diamond Sūtra*, 3. Red Pine's rendering, as follows, is slightly different from the Chinese source I used: "And though I thus liberate countless beings, not a single being is liberated. And why not? Subhuti, a bodhisattva who creates the perception of a being cannot be called a 'bodhisattva.' And why not? Subhuti, no one can be called bodhisattva who creates the perception of a self or who creates the perception of a being, a life, or a soul."

19. Ibid. Red Pine: "Moreover, Subhuti, when bodhisattvas give a gift, they should not be attached to a thing. When they give a gift, they should not be attached to anything at all. They should not be attached to a sight when they give a gift. Nor should they be attached to a sound, a smell, a taste, a touch, or a dharma when they give a gift."

20. Ibid. Red Pine: "Since the possession of attributes is an illusion, Subhuti, and no possession of attributes is no illusion, by means of attributes that are no attributes the Tathāgata can, indeed, be seen."

21. *Hanguk Pulgyo Chŏnsŏ*, Book 7, 634, column c. This book (#7) is entitled "Sŏnga gugam," and was written by Hyu Chŏng. The story about Hui-neng also appears in Sŏ Sahn, *The Mirror of Zen*, 4.

22. *Hanguk Pulgyo Chŏnsŏ*, Book 7, 675, column b.

23. *Pojo Chŏnsŏ*, 420. This inscription, titled "Pulil Pojokuksa pimyŭng" ("Stone Inscription for Chinul"), was written by Kim Kunsu.

24. Robert Buswell, *The Korean Approach to Zen*, 242.

25. Ibid., 253.

26. *Pojo Chŏnsŏ*, 420.

27. Robert Buswell, *The Korean Approach to Zen*, 252–53.

28. Ibid., 253.

29. Ibid.

30. Wing-tsit Chan, *A Source Book in Chinese Philosophy*, 18.

CHAPTER FOUR. PRESENT-DAY APPLICATIONS

1. Yoshito Hakeda, *The Awakening of Faith*, 35.
2. Ibid.
3. Buswell, *The Korean Approach to Zen*, 240.
4. Ibid., 252.
5. Ibid., 240.
6. Ibid., 239.

Glossary of Terms

Chinese = Ch   Korean = K   Japanese = J   Sanskrit = S

ākāśa (S): all-pervasive space

anātman (S): no-self

anitya (S): impermanence

āśraya parāvṛtti (S): "transformation of the basis," reflecting the understanding that the practitioner must be transformed for enlightenment to occur. Seen from a higher level, no such transformation takes place, for he is inherently enlightened. On a biological level, this transformation is constantly occurring.

Asvaghoṣa: second-century Indian scholar who wrote *The Awakening of Mahāyāna Faith*, a noted Buddhist text that asserts the nonduality of all existence

Avatamsaka Sūtra: core sūtra of the Chinese Hua-yen school of Buddhism, which asserts the unobstructed interpenetration of all phenomena.

avidyā (S): ignorance, one of the three poisons in Buddhism

bhumi (S): one of a series of stages that an aspirant must pass through in order to attain enlightenment. Major teaching of the Hua-yen sūtra

bodhi (S): wisdom

bodhicitta (S): wisdom mind

Bodhidharma: known as the founder of the Zen school of Buddhism. Born in India, he introduced Zen to China in the sixth century AD

bodhisattva (S): a practitioner of Mahāyāna Buddhism, who places his own enlightenment experience aside in order to help others attain enlightenment

buddhadharma (S): Buddhist teaching or Buddhist truth

Buddha-nature: the nature of Buddha, which is found everywhere, including all sentient beings. Therefore, everyone is a Buddha.

cheng-i (Ch): a designation given to a Buddhist text signifying its approval by an enlightened monk

chih/kuan (Ch): the meditative practice of quieting the mind and observing the field of consciousness

dharma (S): truth, law, teaching, thing

dhyāna/prajñā (S): see chih/kuan above. This term is used frequently by Zen Buddhists emptiness: the experience of anātman or no-self. This is explained through the theory of dependent origination (see pratītya samutpāda)

Heart Sūtra: popular Mahāyāna text, which exalts the concept of emptiness, stating "Form is emptiness, emptiness is form"

Hīnayāna (S): term used by Mahāyāna Buddhists to refer to those who do not understand or practice the spirit of the bodhisattva

Hua-yen (Ch): a sect of Buddhism which originated in China and asserts the unobstructed interpenetrations of all phenomena

hŭtjit (K): illusory or meaningless behavior

hwadu (K): a question that blocks the practitioner's ordinary, conceptual viewpoint

i (Ch): "doubt." A necessary requirement for Zen practice using the hwadu. Should not have a negative connotation, but rather refers to a sense of inquiry or questioning

i-tuan (Ch):"group or accumulation of doubt," referring to the buildup of questioning which occurs during hwadu practice

karma (S): understood in East Asian Buddhism as a habitual force. Usually viewed as negative, because it traps us, keeping us on the wheel of birth and death, and prevents us from liberation. In the Zen school, however, karma is equated with liberation

kŏjit (K): false, deceitful, or hypocritical behavior

Kuan Yin (Ch) (J: Kannon) (S: Avalokiteśhvara) (K: Kwan-eum): one of the most revered of all the Buddhist bodhisattvas. Embodies both infinite wisdom and infinite compassion. Belongs to either gender, and is known as the "one who hears the sounds of the world"

li (Ch): "principle." A term central to the teaching of the Hua-yen school. Initially seen as opposed to "shih," or phenomena, but ultimately viewed as abiding within all "shih"

Mahāyāna (S): "great vehicle." Refers to a school of Buddhism that views all things as interdependent, and whose practitioners place the enlightenment of all other sentient beings before their own

mom/momjit (K): the body (mom) and the body's gestures or functions (momjit). An ancient philosophical and religious paradigm which asserts the nonduality of all existence. As a logic of nonduality, it is therefore a logic of life

mu (J): a popular kōan (see hwadu) from Japan. A monk asked his teacher, "Does a dog have Buddha-nature?" His teacher replied, "Mu!" Translates as "no"

mukjo (K): muk = silence; jo =bright illustration. Term used for the Sōto school of meditation in Japan. Specifically refers to the meditative practice of quieting the mind and observing the field of consciousness. See chih/kuan

Nāgārjuna: founder of the Madhyamika school of Buddhism; believed to have lived in the second or third century CE. He used a series of eight negations as a means of rejecting all opposites, thus indicating a Middle Way, in which everything is seen as interdependent nāma-rūpa (S): "name" and "form." In Mahāyāna Buddhism, both are rejected as having any inherent identity of their own; they are viewed as ultimately empty

nitya (S): "permanence." In Mahāyāna Buddhism, refers to the nature of the essence of reality, *mom.*

nirvāṇa (S): in Mahāyāna, refers to the state of enlightenment, or unity with *mom*

One Mind: the invisible essence, or *mom.* Discussed at length in the Mahāyāna text *The Awakening of Mahāyāna Faith* as well as in Wŏnhyo's commentary on that text

Platform Sūtra: important text in Mahāyāna Buddhism that espouses the nonduality of meditation and wisdom. Also discusses the meaning of no-thought. See wu-nien

prajñā (S): "wisdom." One of the fruits of enlightenment. Equal to dhyāna in the Platform Sūtra. See dhyāna/prajna

pratītya samutpāda (S): "conditioned arising" or "dependent origination." Key teaching of Buddhism, in which all phenomena are seen as interdependent and thus mutually interpenetrated

Pure Land: world of Amida Buddha. Pure Land Buddhists believe in other-power, as opposed to Zen, which espouses self-power. Pure Land Buddhists chant to Amida Buddha to ensure their salvation

ren (Ch): a Confucian term, meaning "benevolence," "love," or "humanity"

Rinzai (J) (Ch: Lin-chi): a school of Buddhism that relies exclusively on the use of the hwadu

sahā (S): world of suffering or saṃsāra

Samantabhadra Bodhisattva: one of three key bodhisattvas, seen as a symbol of the Buddha's active participation, and appearing prominently in the Avatamsaka Sūtra of the Hua-yen school. The other two important bodhisattvas are Kuan Yin (symbol of Buddha's compassion) and Mañjuśhrī (symbol of Buddha's wisdom)

śamatha/vipaśyanā (S): the meditative practice of quieting the mind and observing the field of awareness. See chih/kuan

saṃgha (S): one of the three refuges of Buddhism, the other two being the Buddha and the dharma. The saṃgha is the group of practitioners who meet together in order to study and practice Buddhism

saṃsāra (S): transmigration. Our human realm of suffering. In Hīnayāna, it is seen as opposed to nirvāṇa, the realm of enlightenment. However, in Mahāyāna Buddhism the worlds of saṃsāra and nirvāṇa are said to be one and the same

shih (Ch): "affairs" or "events," referring to phenomena, as opposed to li or principle. Ultimately, according to Hua-yen theory, shih and li are identical. Furthermore, all shih are seen as not separate from each other

shih shih wu ai (Ch): the fourth and ultimate stage espoused by the Hua-yen school, which states that there exists no obstruction between one event (or phenomena) and another

subul dongso (K): "the enemy is no longer there." Declared by the Korean
    monk Chinul upon his third and final enlightenment experience
Sōto (J): a school of Buddhism, whose practitioners rely far less on hwadu
    practice and more on the meditative pursuit of quieting the mind and
    observing the field of consciousness. See mukjo
suchness: another term for emptiness, reflecting the realm of *mom*
sukha (S): the world of bliss, referring to the state of enlightenment. Also
    seen as an aspect of the Pure Land
sūtra (S): "thread." Teaching of the Buddha, and belonging to the three-part
    Buddhist canon. See Tripiṭaka
taisho (J): Abbreviated Japanese term for the Buddhist scriptures. The complete
    term is "taisho shinshu daizukyo"
t'an-t'ien (Ch): "red field." Refers to an area of the body which is one and a
    half inches below the navel. Believed by followers of Eastern thought to
    be the storehouse for all our energy. Many Buddhist practices involve
    focusing one's breath and/or attention on this area
tao (Ch): "way." When capitalized (Tao), one of the three main philosophi-
    cal systems of the Eastern world, the other two being Buddhism and
    Confucianism. Early Zen translators used Taoist terms in interpreting
    Zen experience
tathāgata (S): "the awakened one;" name given to the Buddha
tathatā (S): "suchness," referring to the realm of *mom*
t'i-yung (Ch): "essence-function"; a term similar in meaning to *mom-momjit*,
    but more abstract. Reflects the nonduality of all existence
ting/hui (Ch): a term similar in meaning to chih/kuan, referring to the
    meditative practice of quieting the mind and observing the field of
    consciousness
Tripiṭaka (S): "three baskets," referring to the three-part canon of Buddhist
    scriptures, which includes the rules of discipline, the sūtras, and the
    philosophical teachings
tzu-ran (Ch): "nature" or "self-so," one of whose characteristics is no-action
    or non-activity. See wu-wei
upamā (S): "simile"; a pedagogical device used by the Buddha and later
    writers or sages to convey an important teaching
upameya (S): "dharma," "message," "teaching." A pedagogical device often
    used concurrently with upamā. It is a message that is clarified by the
    upamā. In the well-known metaphor of a finger pointing to the moon,
    the upamā is the finger, whereas the upameya is the moon itself (refer-
    ring to enlightenment)
vajra (S): "diamond." As reflected in the title of the Vajrasamādhi Sūtra,
    it points to the practitioner's need to be firm and unyielding, like a
    diamond, in his spiritual practice
wu (Ch): "no" or "nothing"
wu ai (Ch): "interpenetrating," that is, no obstruction. See shih shih wu ai
wu-nien (Ch): literally translates as "no thinking" or "no thought," yet more
    correctly understood in Mahāyāna Buddhism as "no dualistic thought,"
    which is the thought of the Buddha

wu-wei (Ch): "no action" or "non-activity." An important term in Taoism

yadan pŏpsŭk (K): "dharma seat in the wild field," referring to gatherings of Buddhist practitioners during the ancient Koryo dynasty in Korea. The meaning has now degenerated to mean "noisy"

yŏsu dongso (K): "staying with the enemy"; term used by the monk Chinul to describe his inner state before his enlightenment experience

yüan-rung (Ch): "perfect amalgamation," referring to both the sacred and profane realms of phenomena, which are open to all the influences of the universe

yŭmbul (K): chanting practice in Korea that pays homage to Amida Buddha in the Pure Land school. Called nembutsu in Japan

Zen (J) (Ch: ch'an) (K: sŏn) (S: dhyāna): meditation. In Zen Buddhism, the word "Zen" means the nonduality of all existence

Bibliography

Boep Joeng, translator (from Chinese to Korean), and Hyon Gak, translator (from Korean to English). *The Mirror of Zen.* Boston: Shambhala, 2006.

Buswell, Robert, translator and commentator. *Cultivating Original Enlightenment: Wŏnhyo's Exposition of the Vajrasamādhi Sūtra.* Honolulu: University of Hawaii Press, 2007.

Buswell, Robert. *The Formation of Ch'an Ideology in China and Korea.* Princeton: Princeton University Press, 1989.

————. *The Korean Approach to Zen: The Collected Works of Chinul.* Honolulu: University of Hawaii Press, 1983.

Chan, Wing-tsit, translator and compiler. *A Source Book in Chinese Philosophy.* Princeton: Princeton University Press, 1963.

Hakeda, Yoshito S., translator and commentator. *The Awakening of Faith.* New York: Columbia University Press, 2006.

Han'guk Pulgyo Chŏnsŏ (Entire Collection of Korean Buddhist Writings). Seoul: Dongguk University, 1979.

Lau, D. C., translator. *Lao Tzu: Tao te Ching.* New York: Penguin Putnam, 1963.

————, *Mencius.* New York: Penguin Group, 2003.

Lee, Peter H., editor. *Sourcebook of Korean Civilization, Volume I.* New York: Columbia University Press, 1993.

Legge, James, translator and commentator. *Confucius: Analects, The Great Learning, and the Doctrine of the Mean.* New York: Dover, 1971.

————. *The Works of Mencius.* New York: Dover, 1970.

Park, Sung Bae. *Buddhist Faith and Sudden Enlightenment.* Albany: State University of New York Press, 1983.

Park, Sung Bae, translator and commentator. *Wŏnhyo's Commentary on the Awakening of Mahāyāna Faith.* To be published.

Pojo Chŏnsŏ (Entire Collection of Chinul's Writings). Chŏnnam: Songgwangsa, 1989.

Red Pine, translator and commentator. *The Diamond Sūtra.* New York: Counterpoint, 2001.

————. *The Heart Sūtra.* Washington, DC: Shoemaker and Hoard, 2004.

Waley, Arthur, translator and commentator. *The Way and Its Power.* New York: Grove Press, 1958.

Yampolsky, Philip B., translator and commentator. *The Platform Sūtra of the Sixth Patriarch.* New York: Columbia University Press, 1967.

Index

147